A GUIDE TO INDEPENDENT LIVING

A GUIDE TO INDEPENDENT LIVING

Jane Libman Nemiroff

Butterick Publishing

Copyright © 1980 by Butterick Publishing, A Division of American Can Company.

All rights reserved. No part of this work may be reproduced in any form by any means without permission in writing from the publisher, except by a reviewer who may quote brief passages in a review.

LIBRARY OF CONGRESS CATALOG CARD NO.: 80-69403

Nemiroff, Jane
    A Guide to Independent Living

NY: Butterick Publishing Co.
224 p.
8010   800820

ISBN 0-88421-820-1

Printed in the U.S.A.

10 9 8 7 6 5 4 3 2 1   1985 84 83 82 81 80

Cover Design: *Peter Morance*

FOREWORD

Establishing your own independent lifestyle is the adventure of a lifetime. It is an opportunity to be who you are and to decide just what you want from life. In *A Guide to Independent Living,* you can find information on how to live on your own. It gives you facts that will help make your independent life a rich and fulfilling experience.

This comprehensive book covers all aspects of daily living, from finding and furnishing a place to live to buying a car. It includes information on housing, food, nutrition, kitchen basics, wardrobe planning, health, and making the most of your leisure.

A Guide to Independent Living is the result of extensive research into the needs of those people who have experienced the joys, dilemmas, and rewards of newly acquired independence.

CONTENTS

Introduction

MOVING ON

Becoming Yourself 2
Is It Time? 2
Knowing the Costs 3
Setting Up a Budget 4
Computing Your Monthly Expenses 6

1 SHELTER

Finding Shelter 9
Renting a Home 10
Buying a Home 11
Should You Share? 14
Housing Resources 15
What's a "Good" Apartment? 16
Leases: What You Should Know 19
Moving In 20
Planning Your Environment 23
Buying Home Furnishings 24
Furniture on a Budget 25
Buying Housewares 27
Keeping Up with Housekeeping 27
Home Security 30

2 FOOD

Nutrition 36
Planning Your Menu 41
Food Shopping 41
Recognizing Quality 46
Buying
  MEAT 47
  POULTRY 47
  VEAL 56
  LAMB AND MUTTON 56
  PORK 56
  FISH 57
  VEGETABLES AND FRUIT 57
  CHEESE 58
  HERBS AND SPICES 64
  STAPLES 68
Cooking 69
Cooking Methods 79
  RED MEATS 80
  POULTRY 84
  SEAFOOD 85
Serving Food 86
Kitchen Safety 87

3 CLOTHING

A New Look 91
Shopping for Clothes 91
Clothing Labels 94
Caring for Your Clothes 96
Doing Your Laundry 101
Special Care Items 101
Removing Stains 103
Basic Clothing Repairs 106

4 M🪙NEY

Finding a Job   **111**
Interviewing   **114**
Managing Your Money   **115**
Banking: The Basics   **118**
What Is a Bank?   **118**
Checking Accounts   **119**
Savings Accounts   **121**
Loans   **121**
Credit   **122**
Three Types of Credit Cards   **123**
Checking Up on Your Credit   **128**
Insurance   **132**
Investments   **136**
Taxes   **140**
Legalities   **144**
Finding a Good Lawyer   **144**
How to Sue in People's Court   **145**
Legal Aid Society   **146**
Power of Attorney   **146**
Keeping Important Documents and Papers   **147**
Wills   **147**

5 LEISURE

At-Home Entertaining   **151**
Giving a Dinner Party   **153**
Additional Ways to Entertain Guests   **158**
People to Meet, Places to Go   **162**
Places to Go   **166**
Traveler's Tips   **175**

6 HEALTH

Getting in Shape   **180**
Finding a Doctor   **193**
Dental Care   **194**
Other Health Resources   **195**

7 EXTRAS

Owning a Pet   **198**
House Plants   **202**
Buying a Car   **206**
Renting a Car   **208**
One Final Thought   **210**

INDEX   **211**

INTRODUCTION
MOVING ON

Becoming Yourself

Is it Time?

Knowing the Costs

BECOMING YOURSELF

You've reached the stage when independence from others is very much on your mind. Part of planning for independence is self-evaluation. You must decide who you are and where you should be going. People who have failed to set realistic goals often speak of the past with regret. "If only I could be young again!" "If only I could live my life over!"

Planning your independence wisely requires accurate information and lots of help from others. Begin by taking a personal inventory. Attempt to sort out your assets and liabilities (nobody's even nearly perfect), and you will cultivate a very important friend—yourself! If you build on your positive feelings about yourself, you can develop a sense of purpose. But don't get discouraged if "you" don't materialize all at once. Relax—it just takes time.

Think about your goals. Set up schedules for yourself and check them regularly. Remain flexible, too. As you develop, so will new ideas and potentials. You're going to hit a few potholes on your road to independence, so fasten your seat belt. A few jolts won't matter if you know where you're headed, and why.

IS IT TIME?

Making the decision to move on to a new lifestyle is difficult. The independent life seems so appealing. Getting away from it all. Making your own decisions. Doing things at your own pace. Meeting new people and seeing old friends.

But independence from others also means a loss of security, and new responsibilities for you. Are you ready to move on to an independent lifestyle? Probably so, if you can reply positively to each of the following statements:

CHECKLIST FOR MOVING ON TO AN INDEPENDENT LIFESTYLE

	YES	NO
I am earning (or have the ability to earn) a steady living.	☐	☐
I am capable of managing my own finances.	☐	☐
I can adjust to a lower standard of living, if necessary.	☐	☐
I am willing to provide my own food, clothing, and shelter.	☐	☐
I can cope with housekeeping.	☐	☐
I can spend time alone.	☐	☐
I can deal with my emotions and avoid extreme reactions to difficult situations.	☐	☐
I am capable of accepting the consequences of my actions.	☐	☐

KNOWING THE COSTS

Becoming independent has both emotional and monetary costs. Only you can judge whether you're emotionally ready to set out on your own. Discuss your plans with relatives and friends. If they have reservations concerning your emotional readiness to become independent, try to understand their doubts and weigh them as objectively as possible.

If you decide you really are emotionally ready to leave, it's time to compute whether you have the economic resources to do so.

The first step is to figure out how much money you will have available to live on each month if you become independent.

MOVING ON

Setting Up a Budget

A good budget should keep you out of trouble financially. However, you should be able to live with it comfortably.

The first step in setting up your budget is to figure out how much money will actually be available to you for expenses. This calculation usually starts with your take-home pay. Take-home pay, or net, is the amount of money you get after certain amounts of money are deducted from your total, or gross, pay. Some of the deductions are mandatory: federal and, where applicable, state and city, taxes; social security payments (FICA); and federal (FUI) and state (SUI) unemployment payments. Other deductions are those you voluntarily decide to pay: medical group insurance payments, union dues, profit-sharing contributions, and so on. Deductions for Workman's Compensation insurance is sometimes mandatory, sometimes voluntary, depending on the individual circumstances. All these deductions can take a big bite out of your gross pay. Depending on how much you earn and what deductions you claim, the total mandatory deductions can range anywhere from about 10% of your gross pay on up. Until you know for certain what your deductions will cost, keep in mind that the average is about 25% of your gross pay.

Once you have some idea of your actual take-home pay, add the amount to any other income you receive on a regular basis: interest from savings accounts, income from investments, or regular gifts from family. This will give you an idea of your spendable income.

The next step consists of figuring out your expenses. Start by listing all known expenses such as rent, loan payments, and insurance payments. Next, estimate what you expect your expenses to be, item by item, for essential services you have never paid for before. For instance, if you have never lived independently before, you may not know exactly what your normal telephone bill or utility bill will be, but you do know that you will have to pay for them. Estimating without experience is almost impossible, so ask a friend or relative who might know. Continue to make educated estimates of every expense, item by item. The list on page 6 will probably help you.

The third step consists of adding up both sets of numbers, income and expenses, and seeing how they match. If you're like most people, the expenses will be greater than the income. And since this set of figures will not keep you out of financial trouble, it is not a good budget.

The fourth step involves reexamining your expense figures and decreasing them where you can. Unfortunately, this is almost always in the areas of entertainment, food, or clothing. Look for realistic ways to save a little here and a little there. You may find that you can save quite a bit if, for instance, you cut back on the number and length of phone calls you make, or take a bus to work rather than drive.

Once you've developed a budget based on these educated estimates, have it checked over by a friend who knows your personality and who has been independent for a reasonable amount of time. This person can help you spot areas where you can save money, and areas where you will almost certainly spend more than you expect to.

One final word about budgets. A budget that you can't live with is not realistic. Budgets are very personal. They should reflect what you are willing to spend money for, and what you are willing to do without. Your personal budget will be unique.

COMPUTING YOUR MONTHLY EXPENSES

Enter the approximate amount that each item will cost you each month.

Rent or mortgage $ _____

Real estate taxes _____

Water and sewer charges _____

Electricity _____

Gas (household) _____

Telephone _____

Groceries _____

Meals eaten away from home _____

Auto: loan, repairs, maintenance, and gas (not insurance) _____

Public transportation _____

Installments on outstanding loans (except auto) _____

New clothing _____

Dry cleaning and laundry _____

Medical and dental _____

(list continued on next page)

COMPUTING YOUR MONTHLY EXPENSES

Insurance: life and health _____

Insurance: auto and home _____

Recreation (including at-home entertaining) _____

Household help _____

Gifts and charity _____

Savings _____

Other expenses _____

TOTAL $_____

The total you have just computed tells you how much money you will need to maintain your lifestyle each month. The figure does not include the one-time expenses, such as security deposits and home furnishings, that you incur when setting out on your own.

If you're sure you're emotionally ready and economically able to begin the independent life, it's time to think about **SHELTER**.

1 SHELTER

Finding Shelter

Should You Share?

Housing Resources

What's a "Good" Apartment?

Leases: What You Should Know

Moving In

Planning Your Environment

Buying Home Furnishings

Keeping Up with Housekeeping

Home Security

FINDING SHELTER

Finding a place to live is a major step toward independence. You must carefully analyze your needs and assess what's available at prices you can afford.

Answer the following questions to help you decide what's right for you:

CHOOSING A PLACE TO LIVE

List 3 locations you are considering:

_____

_____

_____

Check which of the above locations is your *first* choice.

How close is your first choice to your anticipated place of employment?

_____ Less than 1 mile

_____ 1 to 5 miles

_____ 6 to 10 miles

_____ 11 to 25 miles

_____ More than 25 miles

_____ Not sure yet

Is there public transportation available near your first choice?

_____ Yes   _____ No

How close to your first choice is your nearest friend or relative—someone you can rely on to help you out in an emergency? _____ miles

SHELTER 9

Renting a Home

When you're just becoming independent, renting a place to live is probably wiser and more affordable than purchasing a home or an apartment. Renting gives you more flexibility in case you've picked the wrong location or have to move for other reasons, such as a change of job. There are different types of rentals available:

High-rise Buildings

These multi-family dwellings are generally located near offices, stores, and recreational facilities. There's a lot of privacy in these apartments, but it's often difficult to meet new people. Some buildings have door attendants, a service that increases building security.

Garden Apartments

These apartments are usually clustered and share common entries. Assess the lifestyles of potential neighbors before renting one of these units. Noise and untidiness from others are sometimes a problem.

Townhouse Apartments

These attached apartments have much of the privacy of single-family homes. Each unit generally has its own entrance and backyard. Some have their own cellars and garages as well. They are often more expensive than other types of rentals.

Community Complexes

These apartments may be in any of the preceding types of buildings, but they are rented to individuals with some common interest. There are community complexes for "singles" (usually between the ages of 25 and 35); these complexes have recreational facilities and social programs. However, if "chumminess" is not your style, avoid this kind of rental.

Two-Family Homes

In this type of residence, you are living especially close to your neighbors. Be sure to meet them and assess their lifestyle before signing a lease.

Single-Family Homes

Sometimes "bargains" can be had by renting the home of someone who must be away temporarily. However, a restricted lease and the inability to personalize the decor are only two of the common disadvantages of renting another person's home.

Room Rentals

Renting a single room is usually the least expensive type of rental. Rooms are available in residential hotels and in other people's homes. There is less privacy in this type of rental, especially when kitchens, bathrooms, or telephones must be shared.

Buying a Home

The alternatives to renting involve home ownership. If you are very sure of the location you have chosen and you have sufficient money, you could purchase a house, condominium, cooperative, or mobile home.

Houses

Single-family homes are usually the most spacious and most private type of dwelling. However, they are expensive to purchase and maintain. You can probably afford a house that costs about two and one-half times your yearly income (before taxes). Monthly maintenance costs should not exceed one and one-half times your weekly take-home pay.

Condominiums and Cooperatives

Condominium owners own their apartments directly; co-operators have shares in a corporation that controls their building. Monthly maintenance fees and real estate taxes must be paid for both types of ownership.

Mobile Homes

These provide flexibility with regard to geographic location. However, space to park homes is often difficult to rent, especially in the most convenient or desirable parks, and hook-ups to water and other facilities can be expensive.

APARTMENT?????

CONDOMINIUM?????

PRIVATE HOUSE?????

TWO-FAMILY HOUSE?????

WHAT ARE YOUR NEEDS?

What type of housing do you prefer?

    ____ Apartment

    ____ Cooperative or condominium

    ____ Private house

    ____ Two-family house

    ____ Mobile home

    ____ Not sure yet

How much money can you afford to pay as rent or mortgage each month?

    ____ Less than $100

    ____ $100–$300

    ____ $301–$400

    ____ More than $400

Are you willing to share your home with another person?

    ____ Yes

    ____ No

How many rooms do you require?

    ____ Studio (one room)

    ____ 2–3 rooms (one bedroom)

    ____ 4 rooms (two bedrooms)

    ____ More than 4 rooms

SHELTER

SHOULD YOU SHARE?

There are many reasons for taking roommates—economics, a need for companionship, help with everyday tasks, and so on. But sharing a place to live has both advantages and disadvantages:

PROS	CONS
Someone to talk to	Loss of privacy
Cuts down on expenses	Difficulties in deciding who pays for what
Division of household chores	Conflicts over standards of cleanliness and division of housework
More security	Gives others access to your property
Help when you're in need	May lead to dependency on others

Before you decide to share, learn as much as possible about your would-be roommate's personality, needs, living habits, and schedules. If you've never spent time together, try to do so before making a commitment to share a home. Room together for a weekend, or take a joint vacation.

If you decide to share, immediately discuss the realities of finding and maintaining your home. List the strengths and weaknesses of each of you, and decide who will be responsible for what. Be definite about each obligation, and put your agreement in writing. This agreement between you and your roommate should include the following:

- How will you share expenses? Be specific and make a complete list.
- How will you keep track of your possessions?
- How will you divide the housework fairly?

- What policies do you wish to establish for entertaining guests?
- What happens to your obligations if one of you decides to move out?

If the terms of your relationship are clear from the beginning, sharing a home can be exciting, beneficial, and the start of a long-term friendship for each of you.

HOUSING RESOURCES

Once you've decided what your housing needs are, tap all possible resources to find the right place for you. There are several sources of housing information. Friends, newspaper advertisements, real estate agents, building attendants, and bulletin boards are some of them.

Friends

Very often the grapevine turns up the most interesting and least expensive housing finds, so ask friends to keep an eye out for a vacancy. Let them know what your needs are (location, size, and maximum rent). Try to remain flexible. Inflexibility will reduce the number of leads.

Newspaper Advertisements

This is the most obvious source, and often the most productive. Sunday editions are usually the best, and some of them can be purchased on Saturday night. Buy your copies as early as possible, especially if apartments are at a premium in the area you desire. Number availabilities in order of preference, and pursue them at full speed.

Real Estate Agents

It's their business to know what's available and frequently they know of unlisted vacancies. They'll save you lots of leg work, but they also cost money. An agent's fee is usually the equivalent of either one month's rent or 10% of your yearly rent.

Building Attendants

If you're interested in an apartment building that has door attendants, check with them to see if there are vacancies. You'll find that most of them are helpful. They can direct you to someone who can fill you in on the details of available apartments. Sunday is usually the best day to talk to a door attendant. There are no mail or package deliveries to interrupt your conversation, and tenant activity is usually minimal.

Bulletin Boards

They're not usually a primary source of housing information, but they're worth checking nevertheless. Some supermarkets, local schools, and libraries have them, as do some employers.

WHAT'S A "GOOD" APARTMENT?

A "good" apartment depends on your personal lifestyle and values. When you begin to visit prospective apartments, you must be able to rate them quickly and realistically according to your needs. The following are some of the things you should look for:

Location

Where an apartment is located affects your lifestyle. Living close to your job and a shopping center will save you time, money, and energy. Assess whether you will need a car to get around. How convenient is public transportation and what does it cost? Does the area seem well-maintained and secure? Ask friends about the reputation of the neighborhood. The local police station may be able to give you information about security in the area you're considering.

Apartment and Room Size

The number of rooms depends on your needs and budget. It would be ideal, of course, to have an apartment with a separate bedroom.

In studio apartments (also called efficiencies), all the living is done in one room. Yet there are ways to create areas of privacy within a studio, so don't discount them. The opposite extreme is the apartment with many rooms and, if the price is right, it's hard to turn them down. But don't forget that each room will require interior decoration, and that means money.

Room size is also a consideration. Tiny rooms can be a problem. If they can't accommodate furniture of ordinary sizes, your lifestyle will be cramped. Avoid this kind of discomfort, if possible.

Light

Check to see what kind of sun exposure the apartment gets. Dark, gloomy apartments can be depressing. Plants won't like them, either. If you're shown an apartment in the evening, it's a good idea to visit it again in the daytime before you make a decision.

Ventilation

In the absence of air conditioning, cross-ventilation can provide relief during hot spells. If you want air conditioning and it's not provided by the landlord, make sure the building can handle the electrical load before you invest in a unit. Additionally, make sure you have your landlord's written permission to install the unit. If you buy a unit, remember that walls are natural barriers, so one air conditioner cannot cool a multi-room apartment. Therefore, locate yours where it will do the most good.

Soundproofing

When you inspect an apartment, listen for noises from without (traffic) and from within (upstairs neighbors and next-door neighbors). You can get a good indication of neighbor noise in the early evening when most people are at home. If you can hear them clearly, then they will be able to hear you clearly. To cut down on noise, choose an apartment located away from elevators, stairwells, and incinerator chutes.

Fixtures

The plumbing, refrigerator, and stove should be in good working condition. If they're not, make sure that they will be repaired or replaced before you sign the lease. If the refrigerator and stove don't come with the apartment (sounds archaic but it can happen), make sure you can afford them. More importantly, judge whether the apartment is worth this kind of expense. If it is, you may be able to find some good secondhand buys.

Building Maintenance

During every tenancy there are times when repairs are needed. You can get an indication of what kind of service to expect for your apartment by visually inspecting the condition of the lobby, hallways, and stairwells. If these areas aren't clean, chances are apartment repairs won't come easily.

Building Extras

Sometimes it's the extra services and facilities that make an apartment especially pleasant and convenient. Is there someone in the building who will accept packages when you're out? What kind of storage space is available for bulky items, such as trunks and bicycles, that simply won't fit in your apartment? Where are the laundry facilities located? Is there a garage or outdoor lot in which to park your car, and how much will it cost each month? What kinds of recreational facilities are provided?

Once you've found that "good" apartment, you're ready to sign a lease.

LEASES: WHAT YOU SHOULD KNOW

A lease is a binding contract between you and your landlord, so read it carefully. If you're uncertain about any clauses or terminology, *ask questions.* Don't sign anything until all questions have been answered.

Most leases are standard forms, but special clauses can be added if necessary. Thus, if you have reached a verbal agreement with the landlord or agent about anything (for instance, they've agreed to paint the apartment or replace the stove at no cost to you), a special clause (called a rider) must be added to the lease.

QUESTIONS TO ASK BEFORE SIGNING A LEASE

1. What is my monthly rent for this apartment? When is the rent due? To whom is it paid? Does my rent include gas, heat, electricity, kitchen appliances, or other furnishings?
2. What is the term of this lease? (One-, two-, and three-year leases are common. If there's a strong possibility you'll be moving in the near future, a short lease would be preferable. However, rents are always on the rise, so a longer lease might guarantee you a fixed rent for a longer period.)
3. Are there escalation clauses in the lease that will increase my rent during its present term?
4. On what date can I have occupancy of the apartment?
5. How much is the security deposit for this apartment? (Some states require that this deposit be put into a savings account and the interest be paid to you annually.) Is the deposit refundable, and under what conditions? How long will it take to get my deposit back when I vacate the apartment?
6. What alterations, if any, can I make to the apartment? How often will the apartment be painted? Who determines when any furnishings that come with the apartment should be replaced?
7. Are pets allowed in the building?
8. Do I have the right to sublet my apartment if I must move out before the lease expires?
9. If I have a roommate and both our names are on the lease, what will happen to the lease if one of us moves out?
10. Do I have the right to renew the lease when it expires? For how long? Should I expect an increase in rent when I renew?

MOVING IN

Once your lease is signed, it's time to think about moving. Moving really isn't difficult if you pre-plan and get organized. If you intend to use a professional mover, here's a checklist to help you:

CHECKLIST FOR ORGANIZING YOUR MOVE

_____ Obtained names of movers by asking experienced friends for recommendations or by looking in the telephone directory.

_____ Checked reputations of movers with the Better Business Bureau. Wrote to the Interstate Commerce Commission (I.C.C.), Washington, D.C., 20423, to obtain their booklet about moving tips.

_____ Took an inventory of all items to be moved. Listed all items by name, purchase price, present condition, and current value.

_____ Arranged for three movers to give estimates for the move.

_____ Selected one of the movers on the basis of reputation and the estimate for the move.

_____ Chose a moving date (tried to avoid peak moving periods such as the summer and the first and last days of each month). Cleared the date with the mover and the building superintendents in both the old and new residences.

_____ In preparation for the move, began gathering heavy-duty cartons, old newspapers, tissue paper, heavy cord, tape, felt-tip pens, and stickers for labeling boxes.

_____ Arranged with the utility and telephone companies to begin service in the new apartment on the date of occupancy.

_____ Filed a change of address form with the post office. Sent change of address notices for credit cards and magazine subscriptions.

_____ Began packing least-used items first; heavy items on bottom of carton, lighter ones on top.

_____ Made special arrangements to move fragile items and all valuables, pets, and plants to the new address.

(checklist continued on next page)

CHECKLIST FOR ORGANIZING YOUR MOVE

_____ Finished packing. Labeled all cartons with their contents and the room in which they should be placed in the new apartment. Marked FRAGILE on cartons that contained fragile items.

_____ Packed and labeled a "survivor kit" that contains items that will be useful during unpacking—cups, coffee, soap, towel, toilet paper, and so on.

_____ Arranged to have cash, money order, or a cashier's check to pay the movers with, since they don't accept personal checks.

_____ Inspected the furniture with the moving crew's checker to be sure that the checker's estimate of the condition of the furniture matches your estimate.

_____ Made a final inventory of items to be moved. Made sure nothing was left behind accidentally.

_____ Accompanied movers to weighing station to ensure proper calculation of moving expenses. (This only applies if you moved from one state to another. Moves that don't cross state lines are charged on an hourly or job basis, not a weight basis.)

_____ Received movers at the new address. Checked off all items received against inventory of items picked up.

_____ Checked for damages. If any found, noted them on the mover's inventory list before signing for the move. Then, immediately filed a claim for damages or loss with the moving company.

_____ Began unpacking most-needed items first.

If you don't want to use a professional mover or simply can't afford one, perhaps your friends will help you with the move. Light moving trucks or station wagons can be rented if they're needed.

PLANNING YOUR ENVIRONMENT

Your apartment's decor should reflect your lifestyle. A well-designed apartment can be a source of pleasure. It should be appealing and comfortable.

Before deciding where to place your furniture or what new items you'll need, create possible furniture arrangements on paper. Try to get a floor plan of your apartment from your landlord. If this is not available, measure all the rooms in your apartment and draw them to scale on graph paper. One box might equal one foot. Indicate the position of all doors and windows.

Experiment with different furniture shapes and sizes drawn to the scale of your floor plan. If your arrangements are not well-balanced, you will notice areas in your apartment that appear too empty or too cluttered.

Place your furniture so that traffic patterns are not blocked. Passage from one room to the next, or from one area to the next, should not be hindered. Leave room for doors to be opened.

Attempt to arrange your furniture around a focal point in the room, such as large windows or fireplaces. In rooms where people will gather, arrange seating areas so that conversation can flow.

Coordinate colors and patterns carefully. It's not always possible to remember the exact tone of a color, so take swatches and paint chips with you when you shop. Always ask salespeople for samples of fabrics that you like. Then as you move from upholstery to floor coverings you can coordinate your room perfectly.

Designing an interior takes skill, time, and money. It's a good idea to read up on interior design before you plan your home. Libraries and book stores have books on the subject, and there are many decorating magazines on the newsstands. Also look for magazines specifically devoted to apartment living or decorating on a budget. Room settings in stores may also give you ideas.

If you're still very unsure about arranging and buying

home furnishings, you might take an interior design course or ask friends for help. If you have funds available, an interior designer may be the answer. There are two basic choices: private designers and department store staff designers.

Private designers handle fewer clients and give personalized service. They utilize a great number of home furnishings resources, and will devote more time to the assignment. They will visit your home and supervise work crews if necessary.

There are different ways a private designer can be paid: (1) He or she buys at wholesale and sells to you at retail, keeping the difference as profit; (2) he or she buys for you at wholesale, charges you this price, and adds on a percentage of the total cost as a fee; and (3) he or she estimates the assignment and quotes a fixed fee. Get the method of payment straight before you commission any work.

When you use a department store staff designer, you pay retail prices and must make all purchases within his or her store. Thus, you must be careful that your apartment doesn't acquire a stereotyped department-store look. Nevertheless, the better in-store designers can be helpful if they're not too busy with other assignments.

Whether or not you use a professional designer, have a fixed budget in mind before you shop for your furnishings.

BUYING HOME FURNISHINGS

If you're decorating your apartment from scratch, here are the bare necessities to put on your home furnishings shopping list:

Living Room. Sofa or sofa bed (best for a studio apartment), armchair, coffee table, end tables, rug, lamps, shelves.

Bedroom. Bed (mattress and box spring), night tables, chest, lamp, rug.

Dining Area.   Table, chairs.

Other Comforts.   Clock, mirror, shower curtain, radio, television, stereo.

You needn't or shouldn't want to buy everything at once. It takes time to select and accumulate those pieces that are right for you. Enjoy the experience. You can buy new or secondhand items. In either case, try to shop for bargains. It may take longer, but the results will be worth the wait. Insist on quality for the price you pay.

When shopping for new furnishings, comparison shop. Visit several stores, read advertisements, and consult friends. Try to shop during sale months. According to the Retail Merchants Association, May is the sale month for indoor furniture; June is the month for bedding (beds, mattresses, etc.) and floor coverings; and January is the time for White Sales (sheets, towels, tablecloths, etc.).

Furniture on a budget

If you're buying secondhand furniture or accessories, there are great finds at auctions, flea markets, garage sales, antique shops, and used-furniture stores.

Auctions

These are very appealing to bargain hunters. Not only can you get a good buy, but the bidding system is an exciting form of competition. Check the conditions of sale beforehand. They will be printed clearly in the catalogue or read to you by the auctioneer. A final bid is usually irrevocable, so it's best to inspect all goods carefully before bidding. If you're satisfied with the condition of certain pieces, then bid on them within your means. Prior to auction, write down the maximum prices you're willing to pay and don't exceed them.

Flea Markets

It's great to poke around at a flea market. Hundreds of them are held throughout the country all year long. If you're interested in locating the best ones in your area, ask friends and check the newspaper's marketplace classified ads. A flea market is a marvelous mixture. Usually, you'll find everything from old magazines and license plates to antique clocks and jewelry. If you get the urge, it's permissible to haggle over price.

Garage and Rummage Sales

To find these sales, look in the classified section of your newspaper. You may be surprised at the bargains. Since these sales are not normally conducted by professional dealers, prices are often lower than they should be.

Antique Shops

Good antique stores have great collections of beautiful and interesting items. They're well worth a visit. However, if they're located in high-income neighborhoods, chances are their prices will be more expensive than used furniture stores, thrift shops, or auctions. Nevertheless, window shopping is free of charge, and you never know when or where a bargain will appear.

Used-Furniture Stores

These are a must if you're just starting out and don't have much money to spend. Check the telephone directory for the location of the Salvation Army, Goodwill Industry outlets, and others. Stocks vary from week to week, so you should visit these sources regularly.

Also, don't overlook castoffs from friends and relatives. If you're willing to invest a little imagination and some hard work, these items could be just what you're looking for.

Buying Housewares

In addition to furniture, there are other home furnishings that are necessities. The list on page 28 can serve as a shopping guide. Tailor it to suit your own needs and preferences.

Before you buy flatware, dishes, or glasses, check whether they are *open stock*. Open stock means you can buy one piece at a time—to replace a broken or lost item, for instance. If they are not open stock, you will have to buy them in sets, and that may become expensive for you.

KEEPING UP WITH HOUSEKEEPING

You don't have to keep your home sterilized, but maintaining it so that it's fairly clean and orderly will make life more pleasant. Establishing a routine makes cleaning easier and less time-consuming. One simple routine is to envision your apartment as the face of a clock and clean it clockwise, starting at twelve and ending there. This method will eliminate a lot of extra steps.

How much time you spend at home will determine how much cleaning you'll have to do. Obviously, if you eat out most of the time, dishes won't pile up. In any event, there are some basic chores that need attention no matter how much you may dislike doing them.

Here is a brief guide to cleaning. Follow it according to what does or doesn't apply to you. If you don't get around to doing all the chores, don't panic. The cleaning part of your life is mainly for your sake.

HOUSEHOLD BASICS

Flatware: Forks, knives, teaspoons, soup spoons, and serving pieces. Start with service for four. You can always add more later.

Dishware: Dinner plates, salad plates, soup plates or bowls, cups and saucers (you could use mugs and save on saucers), and dessert bowls.

Glassware: There are many styles and many price ranges. Inexpensive goblets for red wine are a good idea. They work well for serving anything from orange juice to bicarbonate. They can even be used for such desserts as puddings, ice cream, sherbet, or berries. You may want to get a dozen or so. They'll come in handy for parties.

Holloware: Platter, salad bowl, butter dish, salt and pepper shakers, ashtrays, pitcher, serving trays.

Pots and Pans: Roasting pan, saucepan, frying pans (1 small and 1 large), tea kettle, coffee maker, Dutch oven, casserole dish, baking pans.

Kitchen Utensils: Set of knives (paring, utility, and carving), rubber spatula, can opener, bottle opener, tongs, funnel, mixing bowls, cutting/carving board, colander, strainer, measuring cups, measuring spoons, kitchen tool set that includes a large spoon, flat spatula, ladle, large fork, and pancake turner.

Small Electrics: Toaster, blender, hand-mixer, and electric knife (these aren't necessities but they're useful if you can afford them).

Kitchen Linens: Dish towels and pot holders.

Bed Linens: Two or three sets of sheets (fitted and flat), one winter-weight blanket (unless climate dictates differently), one or two pillows, two pillow cases for each pillow, and a bedspread.

Bath Linens: Four bath towels, four hand towels, four wash-cloths, bath mat, shower curtain.

Miscellaneous: Ironing board, iron, hamper, canister set, garbage pail, wastebasket, step stool, dish drainer, cork screw, mop, broom, dustpan, sponges, and vacuum.

HOUSECLEANING GUIDE

DAILY

Make bed. Hang up all clothes. Empty ashtrays and garbage pails. Wash, rinse, dry, and put away all dishes and glassware. Wipe out bathtub and sink.

WEEKLY

Dust furniture, window sills, and knickknacks. Vacuum. Polish furniture. Wash floors. Clean windows and mirrors. Change bedding. Clean bathroom and replace towels. Wash clothes. Defrost and clean refrigerator. Clean oven.

SEASONALLY

Wash blinds and outsides of windows. Clean carpets and furniture. Polish floors.

Cleaning aids help maintain your home properly and make household chores easier. However, a few basic ones are all you really need. Keep on hand the following: pails, rubber gloves, sponges, soft cloths, steel wool, toilet bowl brush and cleanser, ammonia, floor wax, furniture polish, oven cleaner, spray disinfectant, scouring powder, window cleaner, dish detergent, clothes detergent, and fabric softener. An open box of baking soda in your refrigerator cuts down on unpleasant odors.

If you honestly feel that you can't cope with the housework, consider getting some outside help. It sounds more expensive than it really is. Someone could come on a weekly or semi-monthly basis. You may have friends who know of a good cleaning person. If you live in a building that has service personnel, ask the day attendant. Very often, building attendants will be able to recommend someone who's already working in your building.

The hourly cost varies. A one-bedroom apartment can be cleaned in about four hours on a weekly basis. You'll have to compute the expense and decide whether hiring someone is worth the money or whether it would be wise to give cleaning a second chance.

HOME SECURITY

Security precautions help ease the safety fears that sometimes occur when living on your own. Following commonsense personal safety rules and taking simple measures to secure doors and windows will help protect you.

COMMONSENSE SAFETY RULES

- Don't walk alone at night in deserted areas.
- Don't be an appeaser. If someone approaches you on the street, being friendly or diffident won't help. Ignore the person and if the problem persists, threaten to call the police.
- Look around to see if you're being followed when you approach your building.
- Have your keys on hand so you won't be searching for them when you're about to open your door.
- If someone grabs you or your belongings, scream or shout as loud as you can.
- Don't get on an elevator with someone who is suspicious-looking.
- If you're driving alone, lock the doors. Be sure to check the car before getting into it. It's easy for someone to hide in the back seat, especially at night. If you think someone is following you, drive straight to the local police station. Make sure all car doors are locked and windows are tightly closed. If the follower is still behind you when you reach the station, blow your horn until someone comes to help you.

Securing Doors

Securing your entrances begins with the door itself, *then* the lock. If your front or rear doors have glass or wooden panels, the least skilled burglar can knock out a panel and enter.

The safest doors are made of hollow metal. A good door requires a snug-fitting frame. Steel is the best, but a sturdy wooden frame is also good.

If you have a weak door frame or a loose-fitting door that your landlord won't repair, install a jimmy-guard. This is an L-shaped angle iron at least two feet long that is mounted on the frame opposite the lock. The guard will act as a lip that protects the latch and deadbolt from attack, even if the door and frame are spread apart. You can install a jimmy-guard yourself, or you can call a local locksmith.

If your doors open outwards, their hinges are exposed. These can be flanged with a hammer or by welding. Also, a set screw or flat-headed, self-tapping screw can be inserted through a portion of the hinge that is not exposed when the door is closed. You can find these items in a hardware store.

If you have a substantial door, then invest in a lock that will make it reasonably secure. There are many fine anti-burglar locks. The key to the Medeco lock is quite ordinary looking, but the lock is extremely difficult to pick. The longer a burglar must work on a lock, the greater is his risk of discovery. The key to a Medeco lock cylinder can be duplicated only by locksmiths who have invested in a special machine that can decode and cut Medeco keys.

Cylinders with tubular keys are also recommended. Many burglars make fast work of flat-key cylinders by driving a heavy screwdriver into the key slot and then twisting it with a vise grip. This is impossible with tubular key cylinders.

Be sure you have duplicate keys, and give the duplicates only to trusted neighbors or relatives. If you prefer not to give a duplicate key to your superintendent (who must have one in case of fire), at least supply the name and telephone number of anyone who has a duplicate.

Securing Windows

There are two types of windows: accessible and reachable. Accessible windows are those at ground floor level, off a porch, or facing a fire escape. Reachable windows are those that a burglar can reach but only with some difficulty.

For reachable windows, a carriage bolt is a good idea. This type of bolt fits through a hole in the lower frame and into a cavity drilled in the upper frame. The window can be secured in a partially open position by drilling a second cavity higher up in the frame of the upper window. A carriage bolt is not exposed to attack by a hacksaw.

Accessible windows need extra protection. Accordion gates are effective for windows that require no access during a fire. Make sure that your window frame is sturdy enough to hold the gate in place during an attack.

For windows that do require access during a fire, investigate gates that will meet local fire department regulations or standards.

If you feel that accordions or gates are too unsightly, there are manufacturers who make laminated glass and plastics that resist break-through.

In Case of a Break-In

If you arrive home to find a door that appears to have been pried or forced, leave quietly without calling attention to yourself. Telephone the police immediately. Do not re-enter your apartment until someone can go in with you.

Should you re-enter before the police arrive, don't disturb anything. Tell the police what's been taken and how much it's worth. Have your locks changed as soon as possible after a burglary.

If you are awakened at night by an intruder, do not scream or try to apprehend him or her. If the intruder has a weapon, this kind of action may cause him or her to use it. Simply be still, memorize the description if possible, and notify the police the minute you're alone again.

To help prevent burglary and fire, the American Police and Fire Foundation offers the following tips:

TIPS TO PREVENT BURGLARY

- Keep doors, windows, and screens locked, day and night, home or away.
- Burn a light visible from the street at night at your doorway. When away, leave a light burning, preferably with a timing device.
- Never allow strangers or solicitors into your home. Always ask for credentials first, then check them out by telephone.
- Encourage your neighbors' cooperation in watching each other's homes when you or they are away.
- Temporarily discontinue newspaper service or arrange for a neighbor to pick up your mail or newspaper: an accumulation of newspapers is a sure sign that no one is home.
- Learn all you can about crime prevention techniques and cooperate fully with your local police.

TIPS TO PREVENT FIRE

- Do not smoke in bed or allow small children to play with matches.
- Store all flammable liquids in a secure, UL (Underwriter's Laboratory) approved container and in a well-ventilated area.
- Keep your dwelling free of unnecessary clutter and trash. Good housecleaning reduces the risk of fire and enhances your chance of escape in case of fire.
- Make sure your home's electrical system is functioning properly. Do not overload circuits by plugging a lot of electrical appliances into one outlet.
- Drill young children and elderly people as to proper escape routes.

- Learn all you can about your local fire unit and how it operates. Cooperation with fire officials is the best deterrent to unnecessary loss of life and property.
- Ask your local fire prevention unit to inspect your home for potential fire hazards.

When emergencies do occur, it's important to have the following emergency telephone numbers handy:

EMERGENCY TELEPHONE NUMBERS

FIRE: _____

POLICE: _____

AMBULANCE: _____

DOCTOR: _____

INSURANCE AGENT: _____

YOUR BUSINESS TELEPHONE: _____

BUILDING SUPERINTENDENT: _____

YOUR NEAREST RELATIVE: _____

NEIGHBOR: _____

UTILITY COMPANIES: _____

_____

_____

_____

Now that you're aware of what's involved in Shelter, it's time to move on to the next step toward independence— **PROVIDING YOUR OWN FOOD.**

2 FOOD

Nutrition

Planning Your Menu

Food Shopping

Cooking

Kitchen Safety

NUTRITION

Since most vitamins and minerals were discovered in this century, it's not surprising that a majority of people have become aware of nutrition only during the last thirty years.

Although publicity about the subject has been good, occasionally it has been a source of misinformation and food fads. If you want the facts, get a standard guide to the foods needed daily by writing to the National Academy of Sciences, National Research Council, Washington, D.C. 20418. Ask for a copy of *Recommended Dietary Allowances*. It's also available in most libraries. In the meantime, here is some basic nutrition information that can guide you in your food choices while you're becoming independent.

What is a Nutrient?

Nutrients are chemical substances needed by your body for energy, to build and maintain body tissues, and to regulate body processes. The following is a glossary of important nutrients:

WHAT YOU SHOULD KNOW ABOUT NUTRIENTS*
**Definitions are taken from FDA Consumer Memo 76-2012.*

Protein
Protein is the main nutrient responsible for building and maintaining body tissues. Protein forms a part of the enzymes and hormones that regulate body processes, and can supply energy if enough calories are not provided from carbohydrates or fats.

Important sources: meat, poultry, fish, seafood, milk (milk products), eggs, legumes (dried beans, peas, soybeans), peanuts and other nuts.

Carbohydrate
Carbohydrate is a nutrient that supplies energy. It helps the body use fats efficiently and decreases the need for protein by furnishing energy so that protein is used for more important functions.

(table continued on next page)

WHAT YOU SHOULD KNOW ABOUT NUTRIENTS*
Definitions are taken from FDA Consumer Memo 76-2012.

Important sources: starches—cereal grains, rice, and vegetables such as potatoes; sugars—honey, molasses, table sugar, syrups, candies.

Fat
Fat is a nutrient that provides the most concentrated sources of energy, supplying more than twice as much energy, weight-for-weight, as carbohydrates or protein. Fat is the molecular combination of glycerol and fatty acids. Certain fatty acids are essential for good health. Fat also helps the body use other nutrients.

Important sources: meat fats, butter, cream, shortenings and oils.

Cholesterol
Cholesterol is a lipid or fat-like substance. It is important in the synthesis of certain hormones, and a form of cholesterol is converted by sunlight on the skin to form vitamin D. Cholesterol, an essential constituent of many cells, is found in nerve and glandular tissues, blood, and bile. Cholesterol is found only in animal tissues and animal fats.

Sodium
Sodium is an important element in the regulation of body-water and acid-base balance. Sodium, with other nutrients, is important for proper muscle function. Most of the sodium added to food is in the form of table salt.

Vitamins
Vitamins are complex organic compounds, needed in small amounts, that act as catalysts for metabolic functions. (Catalysts are substances that influence chemical changes or reactions while remaining stable or intact themselves.) Each vitamin acts as a body regulator by helping other nutrients perform their functions.

Vitamins are either soluble in water or soluble in fats. Fat-soluble vitamins are not significantly destroyed when you boil your food, and they are stored in your body fat. Therefore, it is possible to take in too much of these vitamins, and that can be toxic. Water-soluble vitamins are not stored in any great amounts in your body. Instead, your body takes what it needs of each vitamin from the food you eat each day, and disposes of any excess through normal excretion, usually in your

(table continued on next page)

WHAT YOU SHOULD KNOW ABOUT NUTRIENTS*
Definitions are taken from FDA Consumer Memo 76-2012.

urine. Therefore, you must have a regular supply of the water-soluble vitamins. Most water-soluble vitamins are significantly destroyed or dissolved when you boil your food.

Retinol (Vitamin A) is a fat-soluble vitamin. It is essential for vision in dim light, and is necessary for the normal health of epithelial tissue, which is the body's first defense against infection. Most vitamin A is obtained from the body's conversion of carotene, which is found in vegetables and fruits.

Important sources: liver, dark green vegetables and deep yellow fruits and vegetables, butter and fortified margarine.

Ascorbic Acid (Vitamin C) is a water-soluble vitamin that is necessary for the formation of collagen, a cementing substance that binds body cells together and that is needed for tissue strength, proper bone and teeth formation, and in the healing of wounds. Vitamin C is also important in iron absorption.

Important sources: citrus fruits and juices, broccoli, brussel sprouts, raw cabbage, collards, sweet and green peppers, potato cooked in the jacket, tomatoes.

Vitamin D is a fat-soluble substance essential in regulating how your body uses calcium and phosphorus. Without a proper amount of vitamin D, your bones and teeth are unable to use these two minerals properly. For this reason, vitamin D is added to commercially prepared milk. Your body normally manufactures vitamin D in the oils of your skin after you have been in direct sunlight. However, the process is a somewhat delayed reaction, so you should postpone washing your skin until an hour or so after you've been in the sun.

Important sources: sunlight, fish liver oils.

Vitamin E is a fat-soluble vitamin involved in the regulation of oxygen use by your body, and is therefore essential to all your body cells. Just how important vitamin E is, and how it works, is still being investigated, but your body's need for it has been definitely established.

Important sources: whole grain cereals, egg yolk, cooking oils, liver, leafy vegetables.

There are at least 9 vitamins in the B-complex group. These are water-soluble vitamins that work together—and with other vitamins and minerals—in most of your body functions. The important thing to remember about the B vitamins is that they work as a carefully bal

(table continued on next page)

WHAT YOU SHOULD KNOW ABOUT NUTRIENTS*
Definitions are taken from FDA Consumer Memo 76-2012.

anced group. If you take in an excess of any one, it won't improve the group's performance, and your body will simply wash away the excess amount. If you take in too little of any one, the group's performance may be slowed or, in extreme cases, even stopped (until the deficiency is made up). Listed below are some of the B vitamins, with their new (word) names and their old (number) names.

Thiamin (B-1) is a water-soluble vitamin that helps the body use oxygen to obtain energy from food, aids the normal working of the nervous system, and is important in proper growth and digestion.

Important sources: pork, heart, liver, kidney, dried beans and peas, whole grain and enriched breads, cereals.

Riboflavin (B-2) is a water-soluble vitamin that helps the cells use hydrogen to produce energy and helps keep skin and eyes healthy. Therefore, it is essential to many body tissues.

Important sources: milk, liver, kidney, heart, meat, eggs, dark leafy greens.

Niacin (B-3) is a water-soluble vitamin that helps the body both to store energy and to convert glucose to energy. In an emergency, your body can manufacture niacin from high-quality protein.

Important sources: liver, meat, whole grain or enriched bread, cereals.

Pyridoxine (B-6) is an ingredient in the substances (called enzymes) that allow your body to use amino acids, the building blocks of protein. Among other functions, pyridoxine is active in the creation of hormones, antibodies against infections, and healthy red blood cells.

Important sources: liver, meat, whole grain cereals, dark leafy vegetables.

Pantothenic Acid, a B vitamin without a number name, forms part of a substance called Coenzyme A, one of the master control enzymes in your body. There is some indication that Pantothenic Acid is made by your body.

Sources: found in all naturally occurring foods.

Folacin, another B vitamin without a number name, is an essential part of the process of cell renewal. This function makes it an exceptionally important vitamin.

Important sources: liver, whole grains, spinach, oranges.

(table continued on next page)

WHAT YOU SHOULD KNOW ABOUT NUTRIENTS*
Definitions are taken from FDA Consumer Memo 76-2012.

Cyanocobalamine (B-12) is particularly important in cell growth and repair, especially of the nervous system, digestive system, and bone marrow.

Important sources: liver, meat, milk, eggs (is not available in fruits and vegetables).

Biotin, a B vitamin without a number name, is needed for proper growth in general. Your body normally makes most of what you need in your digestive system, but antibiotics can diminish its manufacture.

Important sources: liver, egg yolks, peas, beans, nuts.

Choline, a B vitamin with no number name, is involved in the use of fats by the body and in the transmission of nerve impulses to your brain.

Important sources: egg yolk, whole grains, milk, meat, peas, beans.

Minerals

The essential minerals are simple elemental substances that act as regulators through their incorporation into the body's hormones and enzymes. Some minerals (calcium, phosphorous, and magnesium) are absorbed into the body's structure, particularly its bony structure.

Calcium is the most plentiful body mineral. It is important in the structure and growth of bones and teeth, in blood clotting, and in maintaining the proper functioning of nerves, muscles, and heart.

Important sources: milk and milk products, leafy greens.

Iron is a mineral needed in small amounts. It is a vital part of hemoglobin, the red substance of blood that carries oxygen from the lungs to all body tissues. Iron helps the body cells to release energy from food.

Important sources: liver, kidney, heart meats, dried beans, whole grained and enriched breads and cereals, raisins, dark-green leafy vegetables.

The approximate amounts of these nutrients needed to maintain good health have been calculated by the National Academy of Sciences. They are called RDA's (Recommended Dietary Allowances) and they appear on pages 42 and 43.

PLANNING YOUR MENU

Planning daily or weekly menus helps ensure that you'll be receiving all the nutrients your body needs. It will also save you time (less frequent trips to the supermarket) and money (less waste).

The table on page 44 is a daily food planning guide to help you meet your Recommended Dietary Allowances. The guide is based on the U.S. Department of Agriculture's five basic food groups: fruits and vegetables; bread and cereal; milk and cheese; meat, fish, poultry, beans, and eggs; and fats, sweets, and alcohol.

While you are deciding about what each meal should include, don't forget the left-overs from previous meals. They almost always work well as lunches, and sometimes they can be recycled into a completely different recipe.

In planning your menus, variety is the key. Meals should vary in texture, taste, and color. For example, a meal that lacks spice or has all soft foods is dull, and a meal in which all the foods are the same color can be unappetizing (envision oatmeal served with banana, white bread, and milk).

It will take you some time to collect or develop trusted recipes, so in the beginning rely on the advice of friends or on popular cookbooks.

FOOD SHOPPING

It pays to develop special skills for food shopping. You'll get the best values and the best possible ingredients for your meals.

Food markets offer many different types of foods, and a variety of forms in which these foods may be purchased. Five simple rules for efficient marketing are:

1. Plan meals in advance—if possible, a week ahead, and buy with your advance needs in mind.

FOOD

RECOMMENDED DAILY DIETARY ALLOWANCES

Designed for the maintenance of good nutrition of practically all healthy people in the U.S.

Fat Soluble Vitamins

	Age (years)	Weight (pounds)	Protein (grams)	Vitamin A (retinol equivalents)	Vitamin D (micrograms of cholecalciferol)	Vitamin E (milligrams alpha-locopherol equivalents)
Infants	To 6 mos.	13	kg x 2.2	420	10	3
	To 1 yr.	20	kg x 2.0	400	10	4
Children	1-3	29	23	400	10	5
	4-6	44	30	500	10	6
	7-10	62	34	700	10	7
Males	11-14	99	45	1000	10	8
	15-18	145	56	1000	10	10
	19-22	154	56	1000	7.5	10
	23-50	154	56	1000	5	10
	51+	154	56	1000	5	10
Females	11-14	101	46	800	10	8
	15-18	120	46	800	10	8
	19-22	120	44	800	7.5	8
	23-50	120	44	800	5	8
	51+	120	44	800	5	8
Pregnant			+30	+200	+5	+2
Lactating			+20	+400	+5	+3

Water Soluble Vitamins

	Age (years)	Weight (pounds)	Protein (grams)	Vitamin C (milligrams)	Thiamin (milligrams)	Riboflavin (milligrams)	Niacin (milligrams niacin equivalents)	Vitamin B6 (milligrams)	Folecin (micrograms)	Vitamin B12 (micrograms)
Infants	To 6 mos.	13	kg x 2.2	35	0.3	0.4	6	0.3	30	0.5
	To 1 yr.	20	kg x 2.0	35	0.5	0.6	8	0.6	45	1.5
Children	1-3	29	23	45	0.7	0.8	9	0.9	100	2.0
	4-6	44	30	45	0.9	1.0	11	1.3	200	2.5
	7-10	62	34	45	1.2	1.4	16	1.6	300	3.0
Males	11-14	99	45	50	1.4	1.6	18	1.8	400	3.0
	15-18	145	56	60	1.4	1.7	18	2.0	400	3.0
	19-22	154	56	60	1.5	1.7	19	2.2	400	3.0
	23-50	154	56	60	1.4	1.6	18	2.2	400	3.0
	51+	154	56	60	1.2	1.4	16	2.2	400	3.0
Females	11-14	101	46	50	1.1	1.3	15	1.8	400	3.0
	15-18	120	46	60	1.1	1.3	14	2.0	400	3.0
	19-22	120	44	60	1.1	1.3	14	2.0	400	3.0
	23-50	120	44	60	1.0	1.2	13	2.0	400	3.0
	51+	120	44	60	1.0	1.2	13	2.0	400	3.0
Pregnant			+30	+20	+0.4	+0.3	+2	+0.6	+400	+1.0
Lactating			+20	+40	+0.5	+0.5	+5	+0.5	+100	+1.0

RECOMMENDED DAILY DIETARY ALLOWANCES
Designed for the maintenance of good nutrition of practically all healthy people in the U.S.

| | Age (years) | Weight (pounds) | Protein (grams) | Minerals ||||||
				Calcium (milligrams)	Phosphorus (milligrams)	Magnesium (milligrams)	Iron (milligrams)	Zinc (milligrams)	Iodine (micrograms)
Infants	To 6 mos.	13	kg x 2.2	360	240	50	10	3	40
	To 1 yr.	20	kg x 2.0	540	360	70	15	5	50
Children	1-3	29	23	800	800	150	15	10	70
	4-6	44	30	800	800	200	10	10	90
	7-10	62	34	800	800	250	10	10	120
Males	11-14	99	45	1200	1200	350	18	15	150
	15-18	145	56	1200	1200	400	18	15	150
	19-22	154	56	800	800	350	10	15	150
	23-50	154	56	800	800	350	10	15	150
	51+	154	56	800	800	350	10	15	150
Females	11-14	101	46	1200	1200	300	18	15	150
	15-18	120	46	1200	1200	300	18	15	150
	19-22	120	44	800	800	300	18	15	150
	23-50	120	44	800	800	300	18	15	150
	51+	120	44	800	800	300	10	15	150
Pregnant			+30	+400	+400	+150	A	+5	+25
Lactating			+20	+400	+400	+150	A	+10	+50

A—The increased requirement during pregnancy and lactation cannot be met by the iron content of habitual American diets nor by the existing iron stores of many women; therefore the use of 30-60 milligrams of supplemental iron is recommended.

NY Times Wednesday, March 19, 1980
Adapted from Food & Nutrition Board
National Academy of Sciences, National Research Council
Revised 1980

HERE'S A HINT...

Vitamin pills and supplements can be too much of a good thing. Vitamins are chemicals that the body needs in small amounts. Most people get all the vitamins they need by eating a well-balanced diet. If your doctor recommends additional vitamins, be sure to take them sparingly. An overdose of vitamins, especially vitamins A, D, E, and K, can be very dangerous!

RECOMMENDED DAILY AMOUNTS OF FOOD

Food Group	Recommended Daily Amounts	Examples of One Serving
Fruits and Vegetables	Four or more servings including one serving of a good source of Vitamin C (citrus fruits, berries) or two servings of a fair source (tomatoes, cabbage). One serving at least every other day of a good source of Vitamin A (deep-green or yellow vegetables).	½ cup of fruit or vegetable. 1 typical unit such as an apple or a potato or a wedge of lettuce.
Bread and Cereal	Four or more servings each day, including one serving of cereal (or five servings if no cereal).	1 slice of bread. ½ cup of cooked cereal or pasta. 1 ounce of ready-to-eat cereal.
Milk and cheese	Adults: 2 or more cups. Teens: 4 or more cups. Pregnant women: 4 or more cups. Nursing mothers: 6 or more cups.	8 oz. glass of milk. 1 cup yogurt. 1 ounce cheese. ½ cup ice cream. ½ cup cottage cheese.
Meat, poultry, fish, beans, and eggs	Two or more servings.	2–3 oz. cooked meat. 1 egg. ½–¾ cup dry beans. 2 tablespoons peanut butter. ¼–½ cup nuts.
Fats, sweets, and alcohol	Use only as extra treats when all other nutrient needs are met.	

2. Keep the menus flexible enough to allow you to take advantage of special prices at the market.
3. Take advantage of plentiful seasonal foods in planning menus.

4. Keep your basic food supplies stocked by checking the refrigerator, vegetable bin, cupboards, and freezer before you begin to shop. See that the makings for an emergency meal and impromptu snacks are on hand.
5. Read the labels of foods you select. You will find ingredients and contents listed in order of quantity, along with a description of the product, information on its use, and its nutritional content.

In order to get full value for your shopping dollar, consider the following advice for coping with grocery shopping:

FOOD SHOPPING DO'S AND DON'TS

Do	**Don't**
• prepare a shopping list.	• shop on an empty stomach, or you may be tempted to make impulse purchases.
• look for advertised specials before you shop. Demand a raincheck if they are not in stock.	• let your market lure you into making trips for advertised specials that they never seem to have. Stores that advertise specials must have adequate supplies on hand.
• be sure the advertised price is stamped on the item.	• be charged a higher price than advertised.
• look for the date stamped on most dairy products and baked goods.	• buy the closest date. Look for the date furthest in the future—this product will stay fresher longer.

(list continued on next page)

FOOD

FOOD SHOPPING DO'S AND DON'TS

Do

- read the labels on all pre-packaged foods, including frozen foods, for net weight, ingredients, and total price.

- check the label on packaged meat (whole or chopped) for the cut it comes from—rib, chuck, sirloin, etc. This must be stated.

- see that the store has a scale that can be easily used. Make sure it is set at zero before your merchandise is weighed.

Don't

- judge amount by the size of the container or box; do look for the weight or content statement.

- be fooled by fancy names on packaged meat. They don't mean anything.

- forget your eyeglasses when you shop.

When you shop, select your purchases in the following order so that they will arrive home in good condition: canned goods, package goods, household supplies, and other imperishables first; then dairy products, meat, fresh fruits and vegetables, and frozen foods last.

Be sure to check your purchases against the itemized register receipts, and re-add the total of the tape.

Recognizing Quality

Selecting quality items takes time, patience, and expertise. Here are some of the things you should look for when purchasing your food:

Buying meat

You can judge the quality of meat by relying on brand name or by looking for the U.S. Department of Agriculture grade. Beef stamped PRIME by the USDA is sold primarily to restaurants and hotels, but there are some butchers who also retail it. The next two grades, CHOICE and GOOD, are widely available at markets. Good has the least fat, and is somewhat less juicy and tender than the other grades.

Avoid buying meats that seem gray, or have large sections of fat or bone. The tenderest beef generally has fat marbleized throughout.

It is important to select the right cut of meat for the cooking method you plan to use. If you intend to roast or stew the meat, you can use an inexpensive cut. When cooked properly, edible portions of the cheapest cuts are as high in nutritional value and as good to eat as the more expensive cuts.

The following charts (pages 48 through 55) show you how to identify the different cuts of beef, veal, lamb, and pork.

Buying Poultry

Poultry is extremely versatile and can be purchased in several forms. Buying whole birds usually is cheaper than buying poultry in parts or as convenience products, such as turkey rolls.

Chicken and turkey are best when they're fresh-killed. Try to find a butcher shop that has daily deliveries from a farm. Next best is quick-frozen poultry. However, once you thaw these you must use them. Don't let them stand too long, and don't try to refreeze them unless they've been cooked first. Cold-storage poultry usually has the least flavor.

Look for poultry that is well-fleshed and has no bruises, crooked bones or tears in the skin.

BEEF

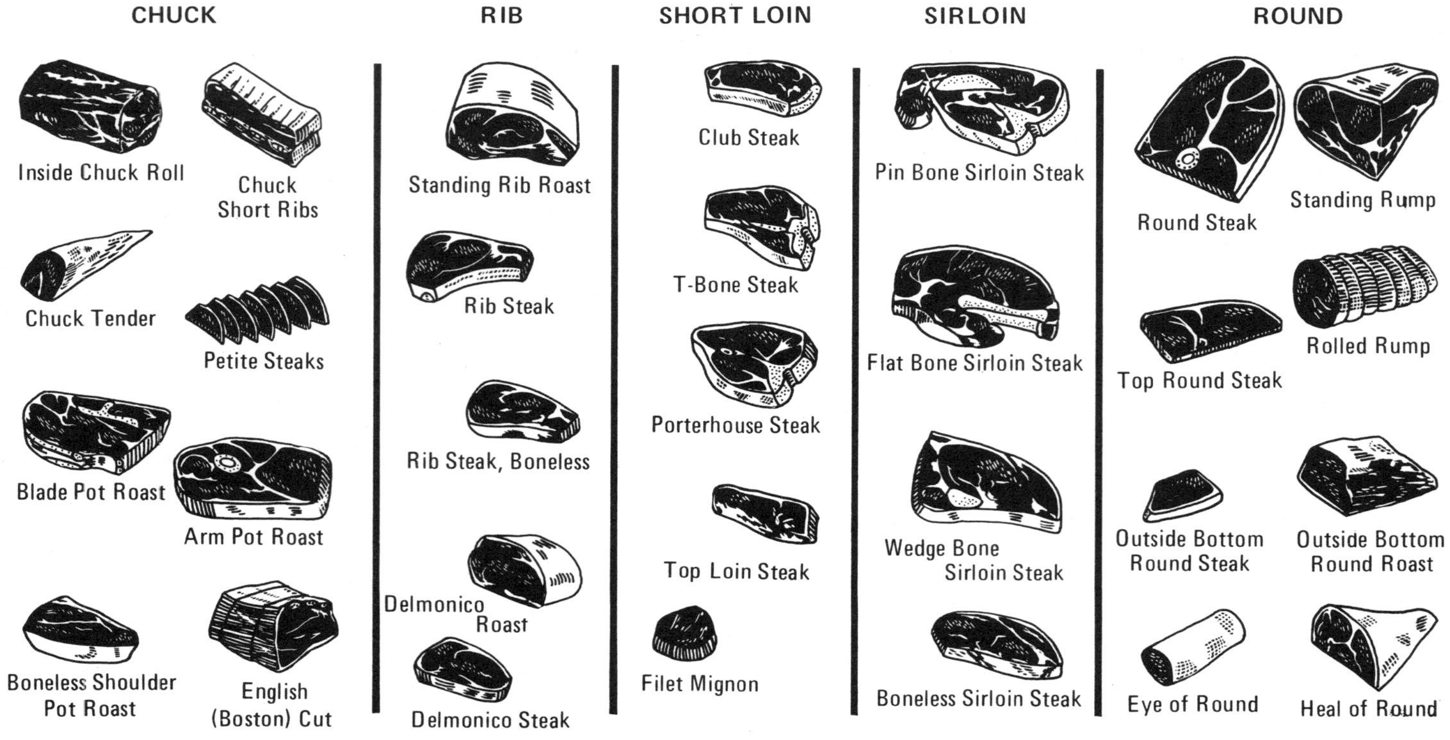

ROUND
- Standing Rump
- Rolled Rump
- Outside Bottom Round Roast
- Heal of Round
- Round Steak
- Top Round Steak
- Outside Bottom Round Steak
- Eye of Round

SIRLOIN
- Pin Bone Sirloin Steak
- Flat Bone Sirloin Steak
- Wedge Bone Sirloin Steak
- Boneless Sirloin Steak

SHORT LOIN
- Club Steak
- T-Bone Steak
- Porterhouse Steak
- Top Loin Steak
- Filet Mignon

RIB
- Standing Rib Roast
- Rib Steak
- Rib Steak, Boneless
- Delmonico Roast
- Delmonico Steak

CHUCK
- Chuck Short Ribs
- Petite Steaks
- Arm Pot Roast
- English (Boston) Cut
- Inside Chuck Roll
- Chuck Tender
- Blade Pot Roast
- Boneless Shoulder Pot Roast

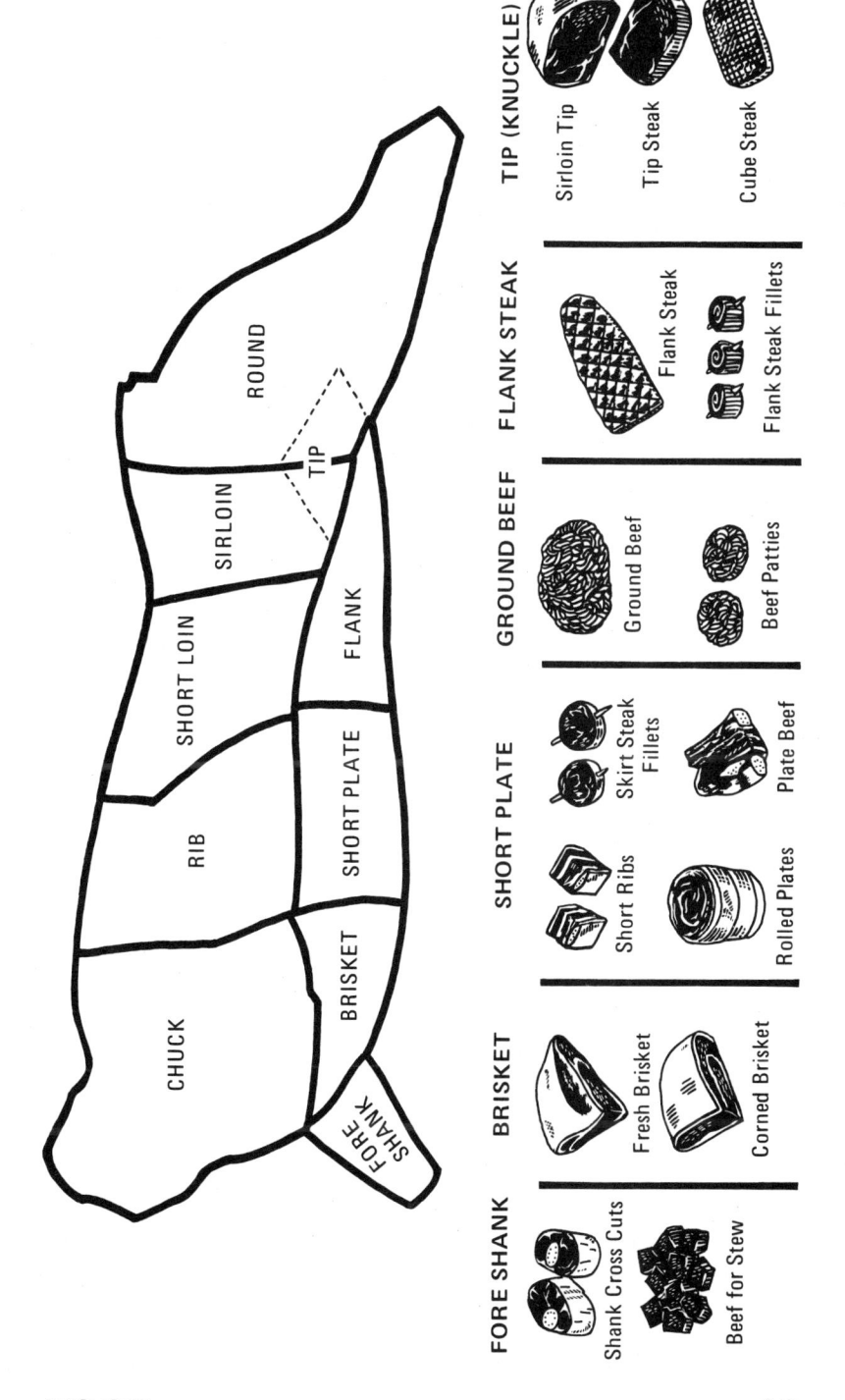

FOOD

49

VEAL

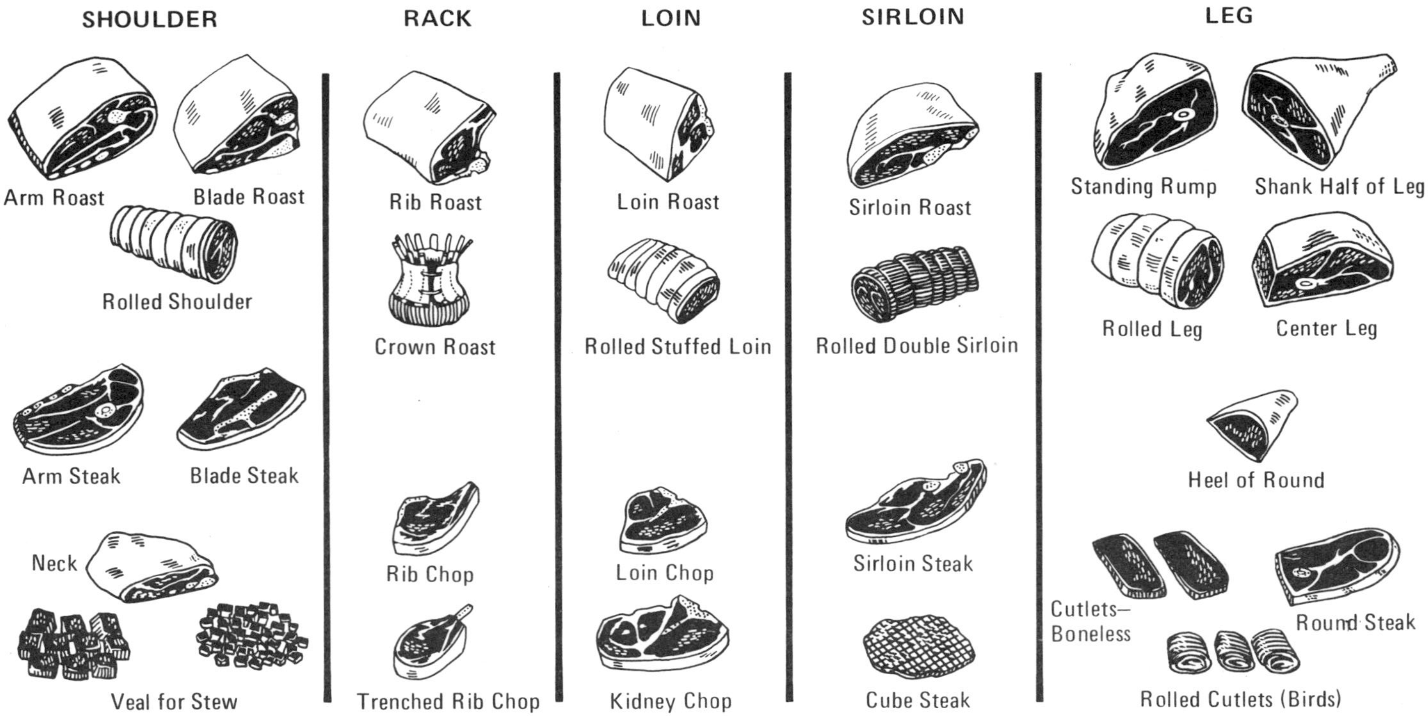

LEG
- Shank Half of Leg
- Center Leg
- Heel of Round
- Round Steak
- Rolled Cutlets (Birds)
- Standing Rump
- Rolled Leg
- Cutlets—Boneless

SIRLOIN
- Sirloin Roast
- Rolled Double Sirloin
- Sirloin Steak
- Cube Steak

LOIN
- Loin Roast
- Rolled Stuffed Loin
- Loin Chop
- Kidney Chop

RACK
- Rib Roast
- Crown Roast
- Rib Chop
- Trenched Rib Chop

SHOULDER
- Blade Roast
- Rolled Shoulder
- Blade Steak
- Veal for Stew
- Arm Roast
- Arm Steak
- Neck

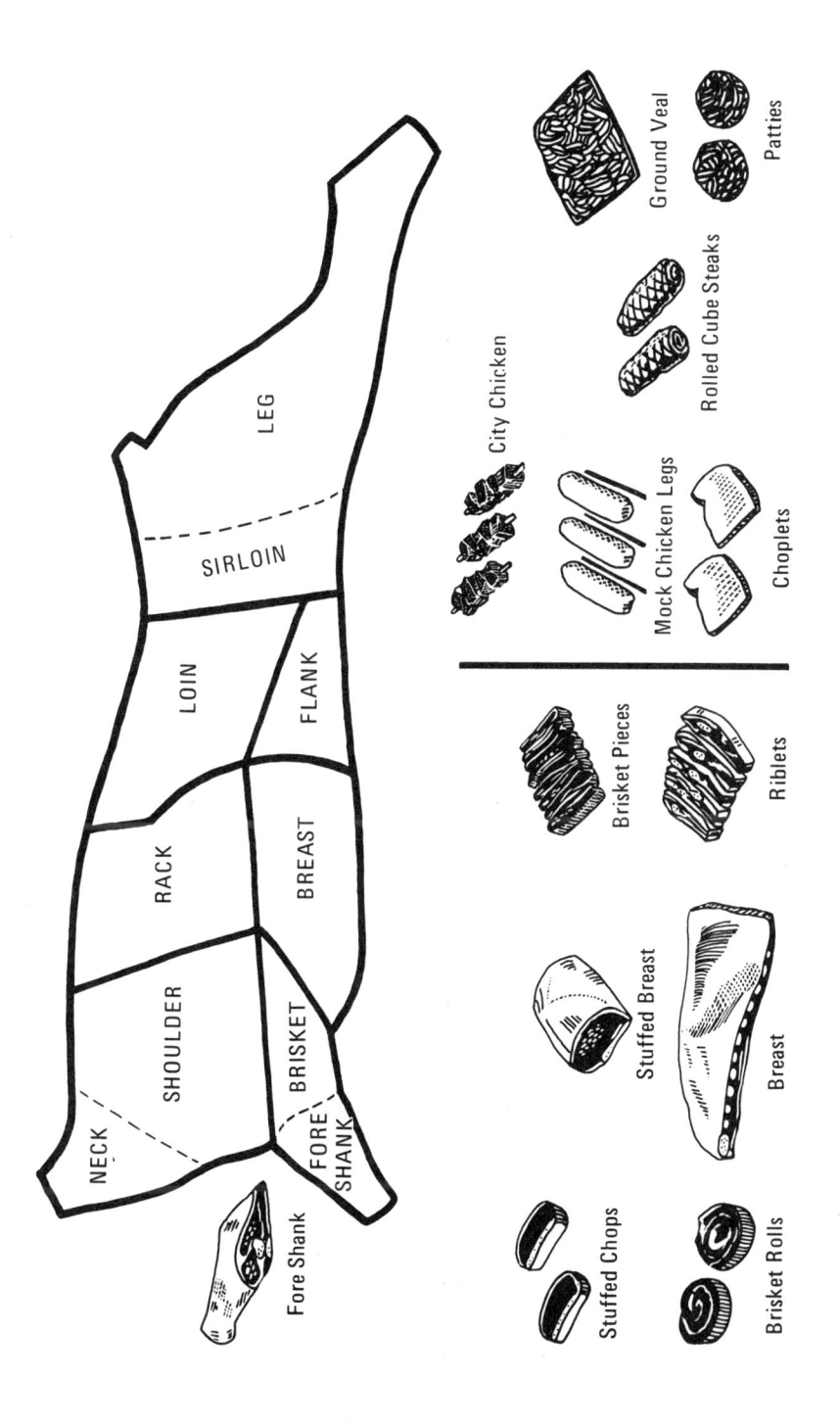

FOOD

Cuts diagram labels:
- LEG
- SIRLOIN
- LOIN
- FLANK
- RACK
- BREAST
- SHOULDER
- BRISKET
- NECK
- FORE SHANK

Product labels:
- Ground Veal
- Patties
- Rolled Cube Steaks
- City Chicken
- Mock Chicken Legs
- Choplets
- Brisket Pieces
- Riblets
- Stuffed Breast
- Breast
- Fore Shank
- Stuffed Chops
- Brisket Rolls

51

LAMB

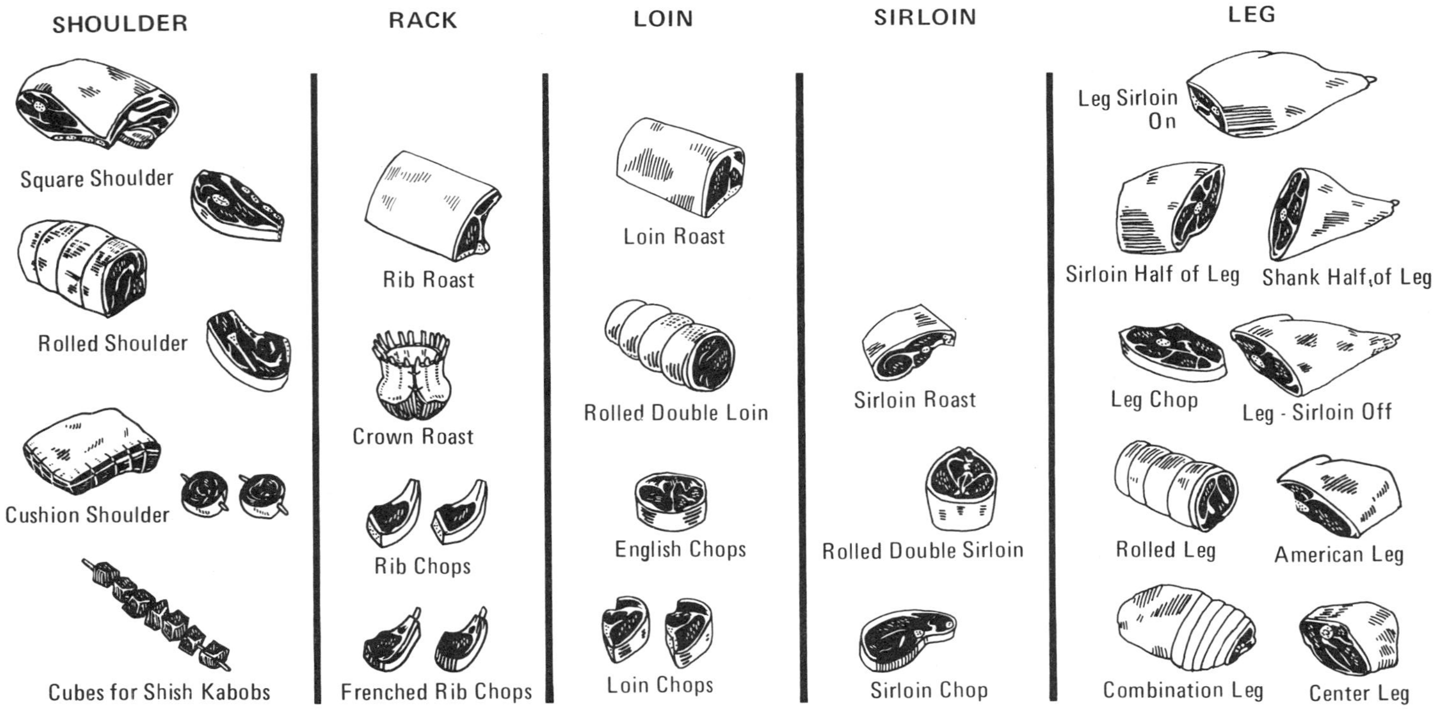

LEG

- Leg Sirloin On
- Shank Half of Leg
- Sirloin Half of Leg
- Leg - Sirloin Off
- Leg Chop
- American Leg
- Rolled Leg
- Center Leg
- Combination Leg

SIRLOIN

- Sirloin Roast
- Rolled Double Sirloin
- Sirloin Chop

LOIN

- Loin Roast
- Rolled Double Loin
- English Chops
- Loin Chops

RACK

- Rib Roast
- Crown Roast
- Rib Chops
- Frenched Rib Chops

SHOULDER

- Square Shoulder
- Rolled Shoulder
- Cushion Shoulder
- Cubes for Shish Kabobs

FOOD 53

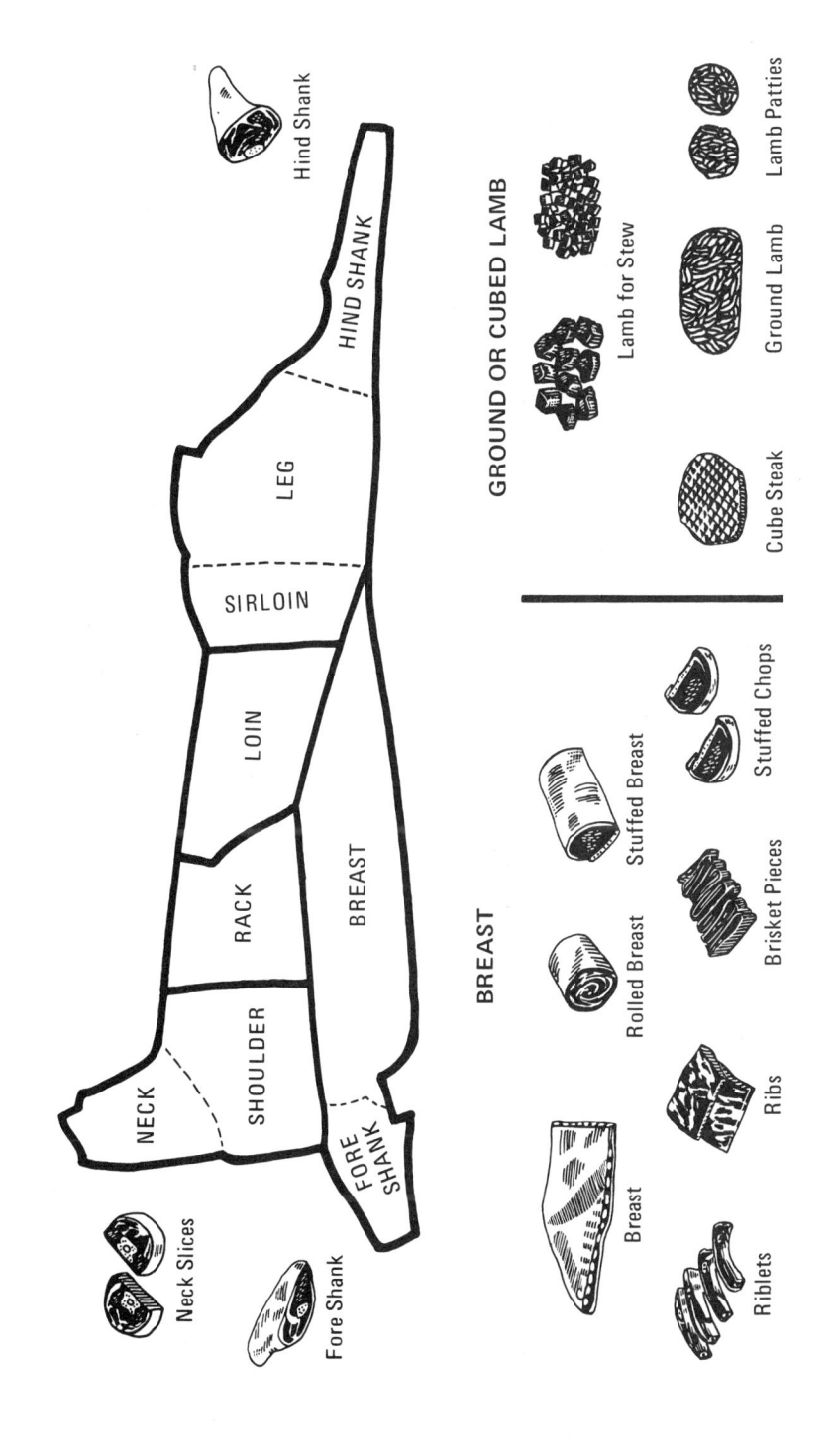

PORK

LEG (HAM)

Smoked Ham, Butt Portion

Smoked Ham Shank Portion

Canned Ham

Smoked Ham Boneless Roll

Smoked Ham Center Slice

Rolled Fresh Ham

Sliced Cooked Boiled Ham

LOIN

Smoked Loin Chop

Tenderloin

Country Style Backbone

Back Ribs

Canadian Style Bacon

Blade Loin Roast

Sirloin Roast

Sirloin Chop

Top Loin Chop

Rolled Loin Roast

Center Loin Roast

Loin Chop

Butterfly Chop

Rib Chop

Blade Chop

SHOULDER BUTT

Smoked Shoulder Butt

Rolled Boston Butt

Blade Steak

Boston Butt

Sausage

Porklet

54

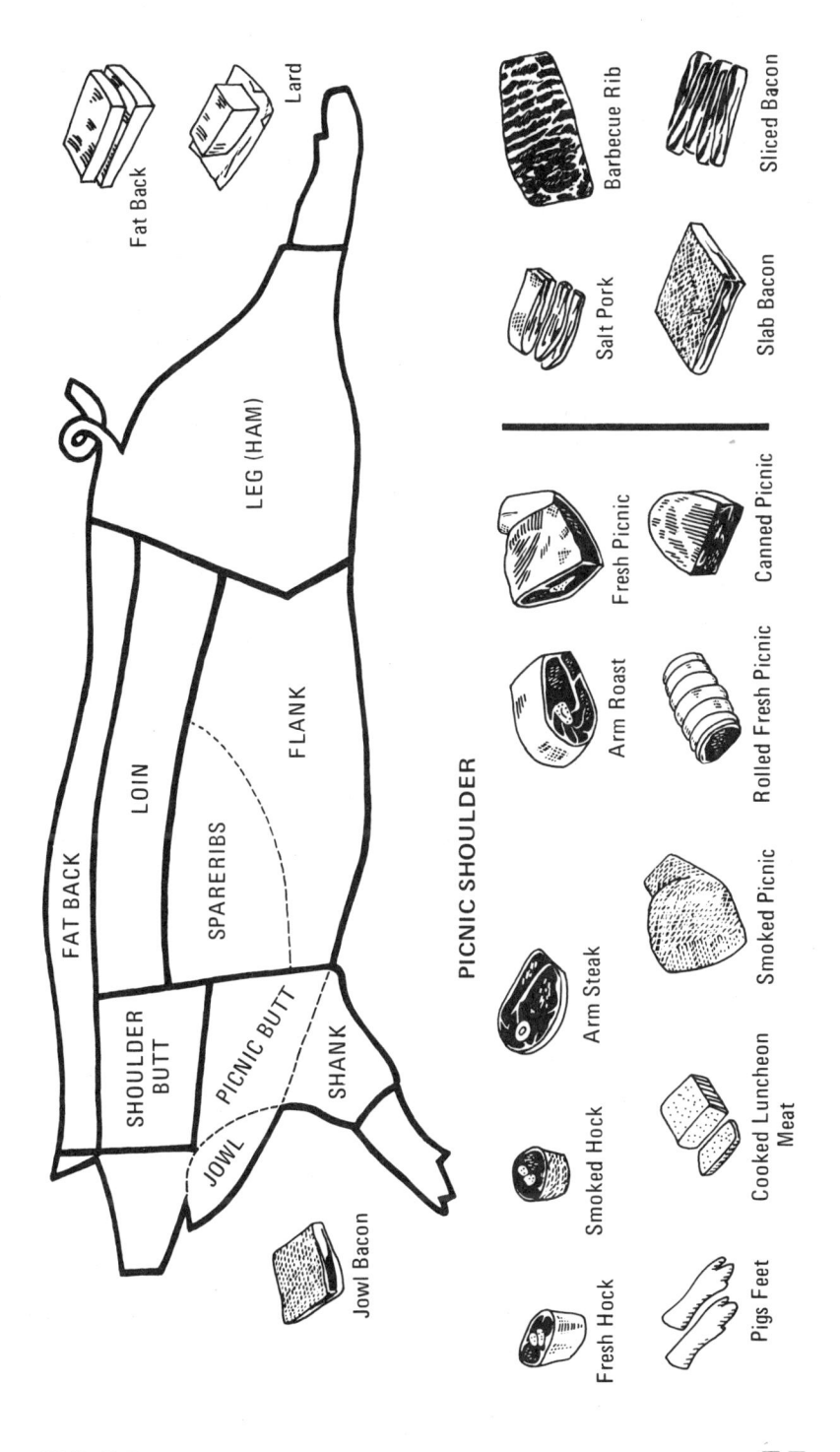

FOOD

Pork cuts diagram:

- Fat Back
- Lard
- LEG (HAM)
- FAT BACK
- LOIN
- SPARERIBS
- FLANK
- SHOULDER BUTT
- PICNIC BUTT
- JOWL
- SHANK
- Jowl Bacon

PICNIC SHOULDER

- Barbecue Rib
- Sliced Bacon
- Salt Pork
- Slab Bacon
- Fresh Picnic
- Canned Picnic
- Arm Roast
- Rolled Fresh Picnic
- Smoked Picnic
- Arm Steak
- Smoked Hock
- Cooked Luncheon Meat
- Fresh Hock
- Pigs Feet

55

Buying Veal

Veal is the flesh of the calf. Tender, delicate veal comes from a milk-fed animal no more than 14 weeks old. If it is older, cooking takes longer and extra seasoning is needed to give it flavor.

Leg of veal is considered by many to be the choicest cut. Scallopine of veal and veal cutlets come from this section. Shoulder and breast of veal are more economical and can be made into delicious entrees when they're stuffed and braised.

Lean veal should be light pink in color and the bones should be porous and red.

Buying Lamb and Mutton

Lamb is the flesh of sheep under one year of age. Mutton comes from older sheep, has a stronger flavor than lamb, and is less popular (but also less expensive).

Lamb is graded like beef—Prime, Choice, and Good. Prime is the finest, but Choice is also excellent. Lamb cuts are similar to those of veal.

Buying Pork

Pork is the flesh of pigs. Young lean pork is light pink; older pork is rose-colored. It is generally a tender meat, which makes pork suitable for many uses.

The loin and shoulder are used for roasts. Pork steak and fresh ham come from the leg. Pork chops come in three cuts: loin, rib, and shoulder. The loin is the choicest.

Purchase one pound per person for most pork cuts, because bone and fat take up part of the weight.

Buying Fish

Fish is low in cost, high in food value, and generally low in calories. It is most appealing when caught in season.

SEASONAL SEAFOOD CHART

All Year Round	Bluefish	Mackerel	Whitefish
	Butterfish	Perch	Whiting
	Cod	Red Snapper	Crabmeat
	Flounder	Salmon	Lobster
	Haddock	Sole	Scallops
	Halibut	Trout	Shrimp
June 1–December 1	Bullheads		
	Catfish		
	Pickerel		
	Walleyed Pike		
April 1–June 1	Shad		
November 1–May 1	Smelts		
September 1–May 1	Oysters		
June 1–August 1	Soft-shell Crabs		

You can purchase fish that is ready to use. It can be cleaned and scaled, and skinned, boned, or filleted. Fish markets will prepare your choice of fresh fish for the cooking method you plan to use.

When buying fresh fish, look for bright, clear eyes, firm flesh, and no fishy odor.

Buying Vegetables and Fruit

Always buy the freshest, most perfect vegetables and fruits available, in usable quantities. Don't buy those that are too soft or discolored.

FOOD

Buying Cheese

Cheese is an indispensable dairy product. Rich in protein, it's not only a quick snack and a good accompaniment for apple pie, it often forms the base for many casseroles and sauces.

Cheese can be classified as ripened or unripened. Cottage cheese, ricotta, and cream cheese are all unripened cheeses; ripened cheeses have been allowed to age under set conditions to develop flavor and texture.

The cheese chart that follows will serve as a guide for your first journeys into the world of cheeses. You're sure to find several that suit your taste. There are many more available than those listed here.

HERE'S A HINT...
Some cheeses should be served chilled, others at room temperature. When you buy cheese, be sure to ask how it should be served to have the best flavor. Brie, for example, is ideal when it's at room temperature and slightly soft, while some cheese spreads or dips are best cold and tangy.

CHEESE

Soft, Ripened and Unripened

Name	Origin	Type	Flavor	Texture	Color	Usage
Cottage, plain or creamed	Unknown	Unripened	Mild	Soft, curd particles of varying size	White	Salads, with fruits, baked dishes, dips, sandwiches
Cream	United States	Unripened	Mild	Soft and smooth	White	Salads, dips, sandwiches, spread, cake topping; useful in cooking
Neufchatel	France	Unripened	Mild	Soft and smooth; similar to cream cheese but with a lower fat content	White	Salads, dips, sandwiches; popular dessert cheese
Ricotta	Italy	Unripened	Mild	Soft, moist like cottage cheese or dry, suitable for grating	White	Usually used in cooking
Brie	France	Ripened	Mild to pungent; distinctive taste	Soft and smooth	Creamy yellow inside; thin brown and white crust	Appetizers, with crackers and fruit, dessert
Camembert	France	Ripened	Mild to pungent	Soft, almost runny	Creamy yellow inside; white crust	Appetizers with crackers and fruit, dessert

(Cheese table continued on next page)

FOOD

CHEESE

Name	Origin	Type	Flavor	Texture	Color	Usage
Soft, Ripened and Unripened							
Limburger	Germany	Ripened	Strong	Soft and smooth with small irregular openings	Creamy yellow inside; reddish yellow surface	Appetizers, desserts, with crackers, rye or other dark breads
Semisoft, Ripened and Unripened							
Bel Paese	Italy	Ripened	Sharp	Creamy with a firm rind; soft to medium firm	Creamy yellow inside; grayish or brownish surface	Appetizers, desserts, with crackers, in sandwiches
Brick	United States	Ripened	Mild to sharp	Semisoft to medium firm; elastic with small holes	Creamy yellow	Appetizers, desserts, in sandwiches
Edam	Netherlands	Ripened	Mild, salty	Semisoft to firm, smooth	Creamy yellow or medium yellow-orange inside; bright red rind	Appetizers, desserts, spread for crackers

60

Gouda	Netherlands	Ripened	Similar to Edam	Semisoft to firm	Creamy yellow or medium yellow-orange; rind is usually but not always red	Appetizers, desserts, in sandwiches
Muenster	Germany	Ripened	Pungent	Semisoft to hard	Creamy white inside; yellow-tan surface	Appetizers, desserts, in sandwiches
Mozzarella	Italy	Unripened	Delicate	Slightly firm, plastic	Creamy white	May be eaten sliced or used in baking dishes
Port du Salut	France	Ripened	Mellow	Semisoft, smooth	Creamy yellow inside; brownish crust	Appetizers, desserts, good with fruit in fondues

Firm, Ripened and Unripened

Caciocavallo	Italy	Ripened	Piquant	Firm	Light or white inside; clay or tan-colored surface	Desserts, snacks, can be grated if fully cured and dried

(Cheese table continued on next page)

FOOD 61

CHEESE

Firm, Ripened and Unripened

Name	Origin	Type	Flavor	Texture	Color	Usage
Cheddar	England	Ripened	Mild to very sharp	Firm and smooth	White to medium yellow-orange	Appetizers, desserts, in sandwiches, cooked dishes
Parmesan	Italy	Ripened	Sharp	Very hard, granular	Creamy white	Used as seasoning
Provolone	Italy	Ripened	Mellow to sharp, smoky	Firm and smooth	Light creamy inside; light brown or golden yellow surface	Appetizers, desserts and snacks
Romano	Italy	Ripened	Sharp	Very hard, granular	Yellow-white inside; greenish black crust	Grated for seasoning
Sapsago	Switzerland	Ripened	Sharp	Very hard	Light green	Grated for seasoning
Swiss	Switzerland	Ripened	Mild, nut-like	Firm, smooth with large eyes (gas holes)	Light yellow, almost white	Favorite for sandwiches; fondues

Blue Vein Mold

Blue or Bleu	United States	Ripened	Sharp, salty	Semisoft to hard, sometimes crumbly	White inside, marbled with blue veins of mold	Appetizers, desserts, dips, salad dressing, sandwich spreads
Gorgonzola	Italy	Ripened	Similar to Blue	Semisoft, sometimes crumbly	Creamy white inside streaked with blue-green veins of mold; clay-colored surface	Same as Blue
Roquefort	France	Ripened	Sharp, slightly peppery	Semisoft, sometimes crumbly	White or creamy white inside, marbled with blue veins of mold	Same as Blue
Stilton	England	Ripened	Piquant, milder than Roquefort	Semisoft, more crumbly than Blue	Creamy white inside, marbled with blue-green veins of mold	Same as Blue

Herbs and Spices

Cooking would be dull without the wonderful variety of tastes that good herbs and spices provide. Since there is such a wide variety of them, it's good to know something about them before you go shopping. And here's a tip: to find out what any particular herb or spice tastes like, cook a little of it in some scrambled eggs. You'll easily see how it affects the flavor of food.

HERE'S A HINT...
Herbs and spices are super...but sensitive. Buy only the amount of herbs or spices you're likely to use within four to six months since they quickly lose their flavor during storage. It makes much better sense to buy a small package of an herb or spice you'll only use occasionally than to buy a "giant economy" size and have it lose all its good taste on the shelf.

HERB AND SPICE CHART

Name	*Seasoning Uses*
Allspice	Fruits, cakes, cookies, beets, marinades, pot roasts, fruit and pumpkin pie, mincemeat
Anise seed	Baked products, cakes, cookies, sweet breads, fruit cups and compotes
Basil	Cheese spreads, tomato juice, minestrone, tomato and pea soup, baked or broiled fish, shrimp, salmon, cheese souffle, Spanish omelet, roast pork, liver, stews, meat pies, roast poultry, fricassee, goose, venison stuffings, eggplant, tomatoes, squash, onions, potato salad, tomato sauces
Bay leaf	Tomato juice, pickling, tomato, beef, and chicken soup, court bouillon for poaching fish, pot roast, sauerbraten, smoked meats, chicken fricassee, roast duck, all venison, potatoes, carrots, beets, salad dressing, tomato sauces
Caraway seeds	Baked products, rye bread, cake, rolls, cheese spreads, cole slaw, cabbage, sauerkraut, pork dishes, pot roasts
Cardamon seed	Baked products, Danish coffee cakes, custard, cookies, pies, baked apples, fruit cup, melon, sweet potatoes, squash, pumpkin
Celery seed	Soups, meat loaf, and stews, fish chowders, clam juice, tomato juice, potato salad, salad dressings, pickles, stuffings
Chervil	Cream soups, omelets, salads
Chives	Egg and cheese dishes, green vegetables, green salads, sour cream
Cinnamon	Cakes, cookies, desserts, fruit pies, hot beverages, sweet potatoes, pumpkin, carrots, pickled fruits
Cloves	Smoked meats especially ham, pickled or preserved fruits, apple, mince, pumpkin pie, hot beverages, pickles, cream of tomato or pea soup
Coriander seed	Banana bread, cakes, cookies, lemon meringue pie

(chart continued on next page)

FOOD

HERB AND SPICE CHART

Name	Seasoning Uses
Cumin seed	Stuffed eggs, cheese recipes, pork and sauerkraut
Curry powder	Curry sauces for eggs, meat, fish, shrimp, salted nuts, creamed vegetables, mayonnaise
Dill seed	Cucumber soup, stuffed eggs, veal and lamb recipes, fish sauces, cole slaw, vegetables, potatoes, sauerkraut, squash, dill pickles
Ginger	Cookies, cakes, Indian puddings, fruits, poultry, pork, Chinese dishes, preserves, beets, and carrots
Mace	Fish sauces, pound cake, cherry pie
Marjoram	Paté, canape butter, spinach, clam and onion soup, broiled, baked or creamed fish, steamed clams, rarebits, omelets, scrambled eggs, cheese souffles, sausage, veal, lamb; meat loaf, chili, creamed chicken, stuffings, goose, venison, zucchini, spinach, eggplant, cabbage, mixed green salads, cream sauces, gravies
Mint	Lamb, carrots, peas, green salads, chocolate recipes
Mustard	Seed in pickles, salad dressing, marinades for meat and fish, powder in sauces, cream cheese dishes, vegetables, Chinese mustard, deviled eggs, ready mix for frankfurters, sauces as above
Nutmeg	Cakes and cookies, stewed fruits, pumpkin pie, carrots, sweet potatoes, beans, eggnog, custards
Oregano	Pizza, tomato juice, tomato, bean, onion, and vegetable soups, lobster, creamed fish, shellfish, boiled eggs, baked macaroni, cream and cottage cheese, roast pork, veal, lamb, meat loaf, chili, stuffings, rabbit, venison, goose, turkey, beans, mushrooms, onions, tomatoes, broccoli, avocado salad, seafood salad, green salads, tomato sauce, mushroom sauce, spaghetti sauce, barbecue sauce
Paprika	Soups, eggs, fish, meat, and chicken recipes, salads and salad dressings, Hungarian goulash, chowders

(chart continued on next page)

HERB AND SPICE CHART

Name	Seasoning Uses
Parsley	Dips, soups, omelets, creamed dishes, sandwiches, salads, salad dressings
Pepper, Black	Any non-sweet dish that needs sparkle
Pepper, Crushed red	Pizza, sausages, Italian dishes
Pepper, White	Use as above where light color is preferable
Poppy seed	Sprinkle on bread, rolls, coffee cake, pie crusts, noodles, salad dressings, cake fillings
Rosemary	Fruit cup, turtle, chicken, pea, spinach soup, broiled and boiled fish, omelets, scrambled eggs, deviled eggs, ham loaf, stews, meat loaf, broiled meat, game birds, poultry, venison, rabbit, cauliflower, carrots, peas, beans, fruit salad, marinades, seafood sauces
Saffron	Adds exotic color and flavor to rice, bread, fish, stews, Spanish dishes
Sage	Cheese spreads, fish chowder, tomato soup, clams, fish stews, cottage, cream, or cheddar cheese, pork, roasts, sausage, stuffings, meat loafs, stuffings, rabbit, venison, goose, turkey, onions, corn, peas, beans, butter sauce for vegetables
Sesame seed	Sprinkle on rolls, buns, cookies, candies, pie crust, salad dressing, fish, asparagus, beans, tomatoes
Tarragon	Vegetable juices, seafood cocktail sauce, consomme, chicken and tomato soup, all fish and shellfish, omelets, scrambled eggs, roast beef, steaks, chops, sweetbreads, stuffings, stews, roast chicken and turkey, mushrooms, tomatoes, baked potato, flavor vinegar for salad dressing, mayonnaise, tartar sauce, hollandaise sauce, bearnaise sauce
Thyme	Clam juice, sauerkraut juice, seafood cocktail sauce, Borscht, clam chowder, vegetable soup, all fish and shellfish, eggs, meat loaf, veal kidneys, boiled meat, game birds, chicken, venison, stuffings, stews, onions, baked beans, asparagus, beets, coleslaw, mayonnaise, mustard sauce, curry sauce, tomato sauce
Turmeric	Egg, chicken, fish, and shellfish recipes, rice and macaroni dishes, potatoes

Staples

Staples are items that are used frequently. Because they have a fairly long shelf life, they can be purchased in quantity. Here is a list of staples to keep on hand:

STAPLES

Long Shelf Life

Baking powder	Pastas—spaghetti
Baking soda	macaroni
Catsup	Pepper—black
Cereals	seasoned
Cocoa	cayenne
Coffee	Rice
Cornstarch	Salt—plain, iodized, sea salt,
Extracts—vanilla	seasoned, onion, garlic,
lemon	celery
almond	Spices
Flour—all purpose	Sugar—granulated, confectioners',
Gelatin—flavored	cube, brown
unflavored	Syrup—corn, maple
Herbs	Tea
Molasses	Vinegar
Paprika	

Limited Shelf Life

Baked beans	Nuts
Bouillon cubes	Oil—cooking, salad,
Canned goods	olive
Corned beef hash	Onion—instant minced or
Crackers	flaked
Fish, shellfish	Packaged mixes
Fruits	Potatoes—packaged
Garlic cloves	instant
Honey	Salad dressings
Jams, jellies, spreads	Sauces—chili, soy, tabasco,
Juices—fruit, vegetable	worcestershire
Milk—evaporated	Soups
instant nonfat dry	Tomato paste, sauce

As soon as you arrive home from the market, unpack your purchases and sort them into groups: frozen foods to go directly into the freezer; meats and poultry to be unwrapped, then covered loosely for storage in the refrigerator or rewrapped for freezing; fruits and vegetables, separating those for refrigeration from those to be stored elsewhere; dairy products, assembled so that they can be carried easily to the refrigerator and stored; and packaged goods, grouped according to where they will be stored.

Work first with items that require freezing or refrigeration. Remember that foods tend to lose moisture or take on other flavors in the refrigerator. Wrap foods for storage in plastic bags or wrappings, or store in tightly covered plastic or glass containers; store vegetables in a closed container or in the crisper drawer of the refrigerator.

The temperature of the refrigerator should be between 38° and 42°. An accumulation of frost on the freezing coils can raise the temperature dangerously. Defrost the refrigerator as often as necessary to prevent this, especially in warm weather or when the refrigerator is being opened frequently. (In refrigerators equipped with automatic defrosters, check the drip pan as indicated in the manufacturer's directions.)

COOKING

Once your shopping is done, you can begin to prepare your meals. Anyone can cook. It just takes practice.

If you're new to cooking or slightly rusty, rely heavily on recipes. Your food will come out fine if you follow the directions and measure your ingredients accurately.

Here are some of the common cooking terms and abbreviations that you'll need to know before you begin.

COMMON KITCHEN ABBREVIATIONS

tsp	teaspoon
T or tbs	tablespoon
c	cup
oz	ounce
pt	pint
qt	quart
lb	pound
l	liter
ml	milliliter
g	gram
kg	kilogram
m	meter
cm	centimeter

STANDARD WEIGHTS AND MEASURES

	Volume in Customary Units	*Approximate Metric Equivalents*
A dash	8 drops	8 drops
1 teaspoon	60 drops	5 milliliters
1 tablespoon	3 teaspoons	15 milliliters
1 fluid ounce	2 tablespoons	30 milliliters
¼ cup	4 tablespoons	60 milliliters
½ cup	5⅓ tablespoons	80 milliliters
1 cup	16 tablespoons or 8 fluid ounces	240 milliliters
1 pint	2 cups	475 milliliters
1 quart	2 pints	.95 liters
1 gallon	4 quarts	3.8 liters

	Weight in Customary Units	*Approximate Metric Equivalents*
1 pound	16 ounces	460 grams

OVEN TEMPERATURES

	Degrees Fahrenheit	*Degrees Celsius (approx. equiv.)*
Very Slow	250°	120°
Slow	300°	150°
Moderately Slow	325°	165°
Moderate	350°	175°
Moderately Hot	375°	190°
Hot	400°	205°
Very Hot	450°	230°
Extremely Hot	500°	260°

In measuring liquid ingredients, such as water and milk, use a glass measuring cup. Keeping the cup at eye level on a flat surface, pour in the liquid until it reaches the line indicating the amount you desire.

Dry ingredients, such as sugar or flour, should be spooned to overflowing into a steel or plastic measuring cup of the proper size and then leveled with the edge of a knife. Never *pour* flour. You will not get accurate measurements if you do.

Measuring spoons should be used for small amounts of dry ingredients. These spoons are sold in sets that include ⅛-teaspoon, ¼-teaspoon, ½-teaspoon, 1-teaspoon, and 1-tablespoon sizes. Level off the ingredients to obtain the right measurement, unless the directions call for a rounded measure. In that case, start with a heaping measure, tap it lightly, and then use the measureful that remains heaped on the spoon.

As you learn your way around the kitchen, you may come upon unfamiliar terms that tell you how to do various cooking tasks. Here, beginning on page 72, are some of these terms and what they mean.

FOOD

COMMON COOKING TERMS

Bake: To cook in an oven.
Barbecue: To cook *over* direct heat, usually over an open fire.
Baste: To keep food moist and add flavor during the cooking period by spooning a liquid or melted fat over it at various prescribed intervals.
Beat: To stir vigorously with an egg beater, spoon or electric mixer.
Blanch: To pour boiling water over a food and then drain quickly—or to parboil in water for a minute.
Blend: To mix thoroughly.
Boil: To cook in a liquid which has reached the bubbling point at 212°F (100°C).
Bone: To remove the bones from meat or fish.
Braise: To tenderize tough cuts of meat by browning first in fat and then adding a small amount of liquid and cooking in a tightly covered container.
Bread: To roll in crumbs, usually of bread or crackers.
Broil: To cook under or over direct heat, under a broiler in the oven or over an open fire.
Brown: To cook in fat until brown.
Brush: To lightly coat the surface of food with a liquid or fat with a small brush.
Caramelize: To melt sugar until it turns to a brown liquid.
Chop: To cut into small pieces with a sharp, heavy knife.
Cream: To beat to a smooth consistency.
Cube: To cut into small squares.
Cut In: To mix fat into flour when making pastry. Done with a pastry blender or a fork.
Devil: To prepare a food by adding sharp seasonings and cooking with a crumb topping. Some deviled foods, such as deviled eggs or deviled ham, are prepared by dicing the main ingredient and then adding the sharp seasonings, but the cooking is eliminated.
Dice: To cut into very small pieces.
Disjoint: To cut fowl into pieces at the joints.
Dot: To cover the surface with small bits of fat, usually butter or margarine.

(cooking terms continued on next page)

COMMON COOKING TERMS

Dredge: To cover the surface of a food thoroughly with a dry substance such as flour or cornmeal.

Dress: To mix a food with some type of seasoning, sauce, or "dressing" before serving.

Dust: To cover a food very lightly with a dry ingredient like powdered sugar or flour.

Fold: To combine two ingredients by turning one ingredient over into the other by using a folding motion with a spoon or spatula. Beaten egg whites and whipped cream are usually "folded" with other ingredients.

Fry: To cook in a pan on the top of the stove in a large amount of melted fat.

Garnish: To decorate a food.

Grate: To cut foods such as cheese or vegetables into tiny particles.

Grill: See broil.

Grind: To put through a grinder or blender in order to cut the food into tiny particles.

Julienne: To cut into long, thin strips.

Knead: To mix with the hands. Bread mixtures are usually kneaded as one of the steps in preparation.

Marinate: To soak a food in a liquid, usually one that contains herbs and other seasonings.

Mince: To chop into very tiny pieces.

Pan-broil: To cook in a skillet with very little, if any, fat.

Parboil: To pre-cook for a short period of time in boiling salted water to reduce the total cooking time. Most often used with vegetables.

Pare: To peel the skin off fruit or vegetables.

Poach: To simmer gently in a hot liquid that just covers the food.

Preheat: To heat the oven before using it, so an even temperature is maintained.

Purée: To make a smooth paste by forcing food through a sieve or food mill.

(cooking terms continued on next page)

FOOD

COMMON COOKING TERMS

Reduce: To boil liquid until some of it evaporates to make a richer, more concentrated flavor.
Render: To cook fat slowly until it melts.
Roast: To cook in the oven in an open pan.
Sauté: To cook in a pan on the stove top with very little fat.
Scald: To heat a liquid just to the boiling point without actually letting it boil.
Score: To slash with a knife.
Sear: To cook very quickly with high heat.
Shred: To cut into thin slivers.
Sift: To shake through a sieve to make the particles finer.
Simmer: To cook below boiling. The liquid used should barely bubble or move.
Skim: To remove surface accumulations such as scum from a liquid.
Sliver: To cut into long slices.
Steam: To cook over boiling water in a tightly covered kettle with the food held above the water, usually on a rack.
Stew: To cook slowly in liquid for a long time to blend and thoroughly mix all flavors.
Stir: To mix ingredients by making a wide circular movement through them with a spoon.
Truss: To tie a fowl with its wings and legs held in place in order to maintain the shape during cooking.
Whip: To beat quickly until puffy.

Recipes also may tell you to include some items that may be unfamiliar to you. Here, beginning on page 75, is a glossary of commonly used ingredients.

GLOSSARY OF COMMONLY USED INGREDIENTS

Barbecue Sauce: A highly seasoned sauce used to baste food cooked over the direct heat of an open fire.

Bouillon: The clear broth made by cooking meat, fish, poultry, or vegetables in liquid and then straining it. Also sold in cube and granular form in food stores.

Bouquet Garni: A small cheesecloth bag of selected herbs placed in a cooking liquid to add flavor while cooking. The bag and its contents are removed and discarded before serving.

Broth: A thin soup; also, the liquid that remains after simmering and straining meats and vegetables. See bouillon, above.

Capers: The tiny pickled buds of the caper shrub used primarily as a garnish with fish or lamb.

Chutney: Sweet fruit pickle.

Compote: A mixture of fruits, fresh or cooked.

Condiment: An overall name for prepared sauces or seasonings (mustard, for example).

Consommé: A clear meat broth, often highly seasoned.

Cornstarch: A powdered starch used to thicken sauces, gravies.

Croutons: Small toasted cubes of bread. They can be made in your kitchen or purchased ready-made in a food store.

Drippings: The juices that remain in the pan after roasting meat.

Fillet or Filet: A cut of fish or meat with the bones removed.

French Mustard: Specially prepared, seasoned French mustards. Dijon is the most popular.

Garlic: A member of the onion family, with a very strong flavor and odor. It can be purchased in salt or powder form as well as fresh.

Gelatin: A powder used for thickening or for forming a jelly-like substance from a liquid such as soup or broth. Also available in flavored versions, which can be added to water to make salads and desserts.

Horseradish: A very strong-flavored plant root available whole or grated and used in hot, pungent sauces to accompany some fish, pork, and beef dishes.

(glossary of ingredients continued on next page)

GLOSSARY OF COMMONLY USED INGREDIENTS

Lard: The rendered (clarified) fat of pork sold commercially and used as shortening in pie crust dough and as cooking fat.

Marinade: A seasoned sauce or dressing in which food, usually meat, is soaked prior to cooking and/or serving.

Meringue: A pie and dessert topping made of stiffly beaten egg whites sweetened with sugar.

Olive Oil: Oil pressed from olives and used for cooking and in salad dressings. It is considered one of the best oils for these purposes.

Pasta: An overall Italian name for foods made of flour and liquid, then cut into various shapes, like spaghetti, noodles, and shell macaroni, and then dried.

Paté: A paste made of meat, seafood, and sometimes vegetables. Used as a spread or garnish.

Petits Fours: Tiny fancy cakes or cookies.

Pilaff: A rice dish for which the rice is cooked with broth or wine and seasonings.

Pimento: A sweet red pepper used as a garnish. Green olives often come stuffed with pimento.

Rack: A rib section of meat.

Ragout: French stew.

Saddle: A cut of meat that includes the entire center section of an animal.

Sauerkraut: Cabbage soaked in brine.

Shish Kebab: A method of cooking lamb (and sometimes other meats) on a skewer. Originated in the eastern Mediterranean.

Shortening: Fat used in cooking.

Soufflé: A puffy, baked mixture for which beaten egg whites are folded into other ingredients, then baked.

Sour Cream: A very thick commercial cream to which bacteria have been added. Used in baking and for dips and appetizers.

(glossary of ingredients continued on next page)

GLOSSARY OF COMMONLY USED INGREDIENTS

Soy Sauce: A sauce used primarily in Oriental cooking. It is made from soy beans and is sold bottled. Also used in marinades.

Spanish Olives: Green olives stuffed with small pieces of pimento.

Stock: The liquid in which a food has been cooked, and often used as the base for soups or gravies.

Tabasco: A very hot sauce to be used sparingly in hot, spicy foods.

Tomato Paste: A thickening agent for tomato sauces.

Worcestershire Sauce: A pungent, brown sauce sold in bottles. Used to add flavoring to sauces, dressings, stews, and marinades.

Gourmet cooking is increasingly popular. Preparing foods that are a little more exotic is easier when you understand the terms used. Here are some common foreign terms you may find in some of your recipes.

FOREIGN TERMS FOR COOKING AND DINING

A la Grecque: Cooked in the Greek style, that is cooked in an oil and vinegar liquid with seasonings added.

A la Mode: Topped with ice cream, as pie a la mode.

A la Russe: Cooked in the Russian style.

Al Dente: Describes foods cooked so they are still firm to bite. An Italian term.

Aspic: A jellied glaze or broth.

Au Gratin: Baked with a bread-crumb topping.

Au Jus: Food served in its natural juices.

Canapé: A toasted or fried slice of bread spread with a highly seasoned food and used as an appetizer. See hors d'oeuvre, below.

(foreign terms continued on next page)

FOREIGN TERMS FOR COOKING AND DINING

Cassoulet: A casserole of French origin. Usually contains a mixture of white beans and goose or duckling.
Champignons: Mushrooms.
Crème: Thick cream.
Crepe: A thin French pancake, usually rolled and filled with fruit or a meat mixture and sauce.
Demitasse: A small cup of black coffee.
Diable: Deviled.
Duchesse: Potatoes that have been cooked, mixed with egg, and then forced through a pastry tube.
Éclair: A pastry filled with custard or whipped cream and topped with frosting.
En Brochette: Cooked on a skewer.
En Coquilles: Cooked in the shell.
Entrée: The main dish of the meal.
Fines Herbes: Herbs chopped and mixed together and used for seasoning. The most common mixture includes parsley, chives, and tarragon.
Flâmbé: To pour liquor over a food before lighting a fire to it. The American term for this process is blaze.
Fondue: A melted food or mixture. Cheese fondue is probably the most common form in the United States.
Fricassée: Braised meats or poultry. See braise under "Common Cooking terms."
Glacé: Frozen dessert; ice cream.
Hors d'oeuvre: Small finger foods usually served with cocktails or other beverages, often before a meal. Called appetizers in English.
Jardinere: Mixed vegetables served in their own cooking juice.
Légumes: Vegetables.
Lyonnaise: Cooked with onions.
Pâté de Foie Gras: A paste made of goose livers.
Patisserie: Pastry.
Petits Pois: Tiny green peas.
Pois: Peas.

(foreign terms continued on next page)

FOREIGN TERMS FOR COOKING AND DINING

Potage: Soup.
Poulet: Chicken.
Ragout: Thick stew, highly seasoned.
Ratatouille: A stew made of mixed vegetables. It usually contains eggplant and tomatoes cooked in olive oil.
Truffles: A fungi similar to mushrooms and used in similar ways.
Vichyssoise: A cream soup made of potatoes and usually served ice cold.

Cooking Methods

Foods that require cooking can be prepared on the stove top, on a grill or under the broiler, or in any kind of oven—electric, gas, convection, microwave, even wood-burning.

The quality of the final results depends on how well you select the proper appliance, the proper temperature, and the proper length of cooking time.

Most ovens made for use in the United States are marked in Fahrenheit (F) degrees. Most ovens made for use outside the United States are marked in Celsius (C) degrees. The charts, beginning on page 80, for preparing meat, poultry, and fish, include both types of measurement.

FOOD

Red Meats

BEEF ROASTING CHART

Insert a meat thermometer into the thickest part of the meat away from fat and bone. Use a shorter time per pound for larger cuts, and a longer time for smaller cuts. Carving will be easier if the meat is removed from the oven 20 to 30 minutes before serving.

Cut of Beef	Weight	Oven Temperature	Meat Thermometer Reading	Cooking Time In Minutes Per Pound
Standing Rib	4–8 pounds	325° F or 165° C	140 (rare) 160 (medium) 170 (well-done)	18–20 22–25 27–30
Rolled Rib	4–6 pounds	325° F or 165° C	140 (rare) 160 (medium) 170 (well-done)	28–30 32–35 37–40
Rolled Rump	4–6 pounds	325° F or 165° C	140 (rare) 160 (medium)	25–30 32–35
Rib Eye	4–6 pounds	325° F or 165° C	140 (rare) 160 (medium) 170 (well-done)	18–20 20–22 22–25
Sirloin Tip	3–5 pounds	325° F or 165° C	140 (rare) 160 (medium)	30 35
Whole Fillet	4–5 pounds	425° F or 220° C	140 (rare)	10

HERE'S A HINT...

Save the salt until cooking is complete. Salting meat before you cook it is a losing proposition. It causes the moisture from the meat to seep out during cooking so that you end up with a dry roast, with far less flavor than it should have. A better idea? Roast the meat to the desired doneness, then salt. The best idea of all? Don't salt before serving. That way everyone can decide whether to salt or not... and today more people are enjoying salt-free diets. It's a healthful habit.

PORK ROASTING CHART

Oven temperature is 325° F (165° C) for all cuts. Pork, often called fresh pork, must always be cooked thoroughly. Pork and ham differ: ham is cured pork and therefore requires no cooking.

Cut of Pork	Weight	Meat Thermometer Reading	Cooking Time In Minutes Per Pound
Loin	2-7 lbs.	185° F or 85° C	35-45
Boston Butt (shoulder)	4-6 lbs.	185° F or 85° C	45-50
Cushion Shoulder	5 lbs.	185° F or 85° C	40-45
Leg (Fresh Ham)	5-6 lbs.	185° F or 85° C	40-50
Crown Roast	6-7 lbs.	185° F or 85° C	45-50

HERE'S A HINT...

Pork must be cooked until it's well done. No doubt you've heard that before, but do you know why? Pork can carry a bacteria which could cause a serious disease called trichinosis. The fact is that today most pork does not carry those bacteria, but since there's no way to check the meat before cooking, the experts suggest you always cook pork and pork products, such as sausage or frankfurters, thoroughly. If any harmful bacteria are in the meat, they will be destroyed... and you can eat pork with no problem at all.

VEAL ROASTING CHART

Oven temperature is 325° F (165° C) for all cuts.

Cut of Veal	Weight	Meat Thermometer Reading	Cooking Time In Minutes Per Pound
Leg	5-8 lbs.	170°-180° F or 77°-82° C	35
Loin	4-6 lbs.	170°-180° F or 77°-82° C	35-40
Rolled Shoulder	3-5 lbs.	170°-180° F or 77°-82° C	40-45
Stuffed Breast			40-45
Shoulder	4-6 lbs.	170°-180° F or 77°-82° C	35-40

FOOD

LAMB ROASTING CHART

Oven temperature is 325° F (165° C) for all cuts.

Cut of Lamb	Weight	Meat Thermometer Reading	Cooking Time In Minutes Per Pound
Leg	5–8 lbs.	165°–170° F (rare) or 75°–77° C	25–30
		175°–180° F (medium) or 80°–82° C	30–35
Shoulder (cushion)	3–5 lbs.	175°–180° F or 80°–82° C	30–35
Rolled Shoulder	3–5 lbs.	175°–180° F or 80°–82° C	35–45
Crown Roast	4–6 lbs.	175°–180° F or 80°–82° C	35–45

LAMB BROILING CHART

	Thickness	Medium	Well-Done
Lamb Chops	¾″	5 minutes*	6–7 minutes*
Rib, Loin, Shoulder	1½″	9 minutes*	11 minutes*

*Time per side.

HERE'S A HINT...

There's more to a lamb than legs. Some people have a definite idea about lamb... it's called leg of lamb roast. That's the only way they can think of to prepare and serve lamb. What a shame. Lamb is available in many forms—ground lamb, lamb chops, rolled roast, lamb cubes. You can use lamb to make soups or stews, casseroles, and many imaginative main dishes. Look up lamb in a cookbook, then try any one of the wonderful recipes you find. It will be a special treat.

HAM BAKING CHART

Oven temperature is 325° F (165° C) for all cuts. Prepared ham actually needs no cooking, but the taste is usually improved if the meat is well-warmed. Follow package directions or the following chart.

Cut of Ham	Weight	Meat Thermometer Reading	Cooking Time In Minutes Per Pound
For Uncooked Smoked Hams			
Whole Ham (Bone in)	8–20 lbs.	160° F or 72° C	18–20
Whole Ham (Boned)	8–16 lbs.	160° F or 72° C	18–20
Shank Half Ham or Butt Portion (Bone in)	4–8 lbs.	160° F or 72° C	35–40
Picnic (Bone in)	4–10 lbs.	170° F or 77° C	35–40
For Pre-Cooked Hams—To Heat Before Eating			
Whole Ham (Bone in)	8–20 lbs.	130° F or 55° C	15
Whole Ham (Boned)	8–16 lbs.	130° F or 55° C	15
Shank Half Ham or Butt Portion (Bone in)	4–8 lbs.	130° F or 55° C	15–20
Picnic (Bone in)	4–10 lbs.	130° F or 55° C	25–35
Canadian Bacon		170° F or 77° C	35–40

FOOD

Poultry

CHART FOR ROASTING STUFFED TURKEY

Size of Bird	Open Roasting Pan Oven Temperature	Cooking Time In Hours
6–8 lbs.	325° F or 165° C	3–3½
8–12 lbs.	325° F or 165° C	3½–4½
12–16 lbs.	325° F or 165° C	4½–5
16–20 lbs.	300° F or 150° C	5–6½

Wrapped in Foil

6–8 lbs.	450° F or 232° C	1½–2
8–12 lbs.	450° F or 232° C	2–2½
12–16 lbs.	450° F or 232° C	3–3½
16–20 lbs.	450° F or 232° C	3½–4

CHART FOR ROASTING STUFFED CHICKEN

Class	Weight	Temperature	Cooking Time In Hours
Broiler-fryer	1½–3 lbs.	375° F or 190° C	1–1½
Roaster	3½–6 lbs.	325° F or 165° C	2–3
Capon	5–7 lbs.	325° F or 165° C	2½–3½

HERE'S A HINT...

Stuffing a turkey is a last-minute operation. If you decide to make a traditional turkey, roasted with stuffing inside, be sure to put the stuffing inside the bird *just before* you put the bird in the oven. Never, never stuff the bird in advance. The reason is obvious, when you think about it. The warm, moist inside of a turkey would be an ideal climate for harmful bacteria to grow and spoil the flavor of the stuffing, or worse, create a case of food poisoning. To avoid any problems, always remember to stuff the turkey just before you open the oven!

Seafood

COOKING METHODS FOR SEAFOOD

Fish	Boiling	Broiling	Frying	Baking
Black Bass		x	x	x
Bluefish		x		x
Bloater		x		
Brook Trout			x	
Bullhead			x	
Butterfish			x	
Carp	x	x	x	x
Catfish			x	
Cod	x	x	x	x
Flounder		x	x	x
Haddock	x		x	x
Hake		x		x
Halibut	x	x	x	x
Herring	x		x	
Mackerel, fresh	x	x		x
Mackerel, salt	x			
Mullet				x
Muskellunge	x			
Perch			x	x
Pickerel	x		x	x
Pike	x	x	x	x
Pollock			x	
Pompano	x	x	x	
Porgy		x		
Red Snapper	x		x	x
Salmon	x	x	x	x
Sea Bass	x	x		x
Shad		x		x
Shad Roe		x	x	
Sheepshead	x			
Smelts			x	
Sole	x		x	x
Sturgeon		x		x
Tilefish	x	x		
Trout			x	x
Weakfish	x			x
Whitefish		x	x	x
Whiting		x	x	

FOOD

Serving Food

The environment in which you eat can make mealtime either a pleasant or depressing experience. Even when you dine alone, you should sit down in an appealing setting. A tablecloth or place mats, a few fresh flowers, and some candles can really raise spirits.

It's up to you whether or not to set a formal table, complete with china, silverware, and stemware. Sometimes informality can be just as effective. Baskets, pottery, and woodenware can make a table exceptionally attractive.

Whatever you decide, remember that the best prepared food can be unappetizing if it's not served properly. Avoid putting things on your table haphazardly or using mismatched items or those with missing or broken parts. Do your best to cut and shape food attractively. Here are some pointers for cutting meat and poultry:

Carving Meats Meat looks better and goes farther when carved correctly. Always let broiled or roasted meat stand out of the oven for a bit, to set the juices, before you attempt to carve it—about 20 minutes in a warm place for roasts, about 5 minutes for steaks. Use a wooden carving board or heated platter large enough to easily accommodate the meat.

For roasts, use a sharp, heavy-bladed carving knife and a two-pronged fork. A long flexible knife for thin slices and a smaller carving knife for fowl and steaks would be useful as well. Meat is generally carved with the grain, rather than against it.

Carving Poultry Place chicken, turkey or other fowl, breast up, on a heated platter with the neck to the left of the carver. Bend the leg away from the body, cut between the leg and the body until you hit the bone. Move the leg slightly to find the hip joint and then cut through at the hip joint. Detach the leg and put it aside on a heated platter. Repeat with the other leg. Cut off the wings in the same manner.

Insert the carving fork alongside the breastbone. Cut the

breast meat in thin slices parallel to the breastbone, beginning above the shoulder-joint and working up.

Divide the legs at the mid-joint and, if the fowl is large, cut slices of leg meat. Separate the collarbone from the breast meat by cutting along the bone. Then slip the knife under the shoulder blade and turn the fowl over. Cut and separate the breast from the back.

KITCHEN SAFETY

Kitchens are so much a part of our everyday life that we often fail to think of the safety hazards they contain. Precautions need to be taken with electric and gas appliances, sharp objects, and even our food.

Ovens are responsible for many household accidents. In the table on page 88 are a few tips to ensure your safety.

All electrical appliances should be unplugged when not in use. Periodically check the cords and plugs for exposed wiring or frayed cords.

If you own a dishwasher, don't turn it on if you're going out. Mechanical or electrical failure might mean coming home to a kitchen full of suds, or worse. Also, if you open the dishwasher in the middle of a cycle, allow the steam to escape before reaching into the washer.

Small objects are also hazards. You can be hurt fishing for your toast if you stick metal objects into your plugged-in toaster. Broken glass demands an immediate clean-up if you want to avoid serious cuts—vacuum the area at once, then wipe it with a damp towel. Knives need special handling. Don't wash several in one handful or store them in overcrowded places.

Carelessness with food can cause illness or even death. In the table on page 89 are some simple precautions.

FOOD

OVEN SAFETY

1. To light a gas oven, first open the door, then light a match and place it near the pilot light opening, and only then turn on the gas.
2. Turn off the oven, burners, and broiler when cooking is completed. Check all controls before you go to bed or leave your home.
3. Keep the stove burners clean. Wipe up spills immediately. Caked-on food is a potential fire hazard.
4. Use thick hot pads to handle anything that has been heating in the oven or on top of the stove.
5. Check the pilot lights on gas stoves periodically to be sure they're lit, especially if you smell gas. If the pilot lights are lit but a gas odor persists, there may be a gas leak. Call the building superintendent immediately for repairs. Do not turn on any appliances, and do not light any flames.
6. Use pans of ample size to boil water and to cook in hot fat so liquid and/or grease does not splash over the sides.
7. If you must leave the kitchen in the midst of cooking something on the top of the stove, turn off the burner.
8. Put out kitchen fires by smothering the flames with flour or baking soda, or by using a fire extinguisher. Water only makes most kitchen fires worse.
9. Open the windows for ventilation while you clean the oven with spray cleaners. Follow the package instructions exactly.
10. Don't store matches, spray cans, or any other flammable materials near or above the oven where they could fall into an open flame or where the heat produced during cooking could ignite them.
11. Don't hang dish towels near the stove.
12. Don't touch water at the same time you touch an electric stove, light switch, or other live electrical appliance. A bad shock—even a fatal one—could await.
13. Don't use the automatic timing device to turn on your electric oven while you're away. For safety's sake, it's not a good idea to use the oven when no one is home.

ENSURING FOOD SAFETY

1. Wash your hands before and after handling raw foods. Wash all cutting surfaces and utensils with soap and water after use.
2. Put all perishable and frozen foods in the refrigerator as soon as possible after shopping. Wrap meats and poultry in freezer paper or plastic wrap and aluminum foil. Uncooked meat that has been properly refrigerated for three days or less can be frozen. Otherwise use immediately.
3. Defrost foods in the refrigerator, *not* at room temperature. Place them on a plate or in a pan to prevent dripping into other foods.
4. Do not thaw and refreeze frozen meats, fish, poultry and vegetables without cooking them first.
5. Store leftover foods in the refrigerator, promptly. Cool them in small quantities and shallow layers so the temperature of the food is brought down to refrigerator temperature in 2 to 3 hours.
6. Do not use any foodstuff that looks or smells bad.
7. Don't use canned foods in bulging cans or with bulging lids on glass jars. If it's commercially canned food, return it to the supermarket where you bought it and inform your local health official. It could save lives.
8. Put prepared foods in the refrigerator until ready to serve. All foodstuffs with an egg or dairy base must be refrigerated.
9. If you have a pet, keep its feeding dishes, toys, and bedding out of the kitchen.
10. Use a meat thermometer to make sure the interior of meat is cooked thoroughly (at least 175° to 185° F for poultry, 170° F for fresh pork).
11. Remove dressing (stuffing) from meat, fish, and poultry before refrigerating. Refrigerate immediately and use leftovers within a day or two.
12. Don't store foods, especially acidic foods (orange juice, for example) in pottery unless you know for sure it has a glaze that contains no lead.

FOOD

3 CLOTHING

A New Look

Shopping for Clothes

Caring for Clothes

A NEW LOOK

When you begin your independent lifestyle, feeling good about your appearance will give you confidence. New clothes can uplift the spirit, but be sure to choose affordable clothes that emphasize your good points and that are appropriate for your new lifestyle.

Part of the pleasure of an independent lifestyle comes from dressing in styles and combinations that you choose and that express the new, independent you. There are a few time-proven tips, however. For example, don't indiscriminately embrace a new fashion if it doesn't suit your body—people who want to hide double chins shouldn't wear turtlenecks.

Suitability is the main key to dressing well. Each body has its assets and liabilities. In the table on page 92 are a few tips on ways to create visual illusions by using clothing that complements your body structure.

People who dress well are usually up-to-date in fashion, but they don't look "trendy." They know how to let their individuality show. Good dressers also know how to go lightly on jewelry and fragrances. Clanking jewelry can be disruptive and heavy scents can be irritating, especially on the job.

Neatness also counts. Your clothes should fit well. If you're putting on or taking off weight, be sure to alter your clothing. Invest in a good hair-cut, too. The best-looking outfit can be ruined by hair that is poorly styled.

To find a look that suits you, observe people, consult with your friends, window-shop, or read fashion magazines. If you're really at a loss, some department stores have professional shoppers and make-up artists who can help you.

SHOPPING FOR CLOTHES

It seems as though we're always in need of clothes. Sometimes, the need is more imagined than real. Before shopping for a

CLOTHES TO FIT THE FIGURE

Build	Men	Women
Short	Choose pin-stripes and thin vertical lines in sport shirts and slacks.	Choose clothes with vertical lines. Heels add height, but don't overdo it. Hairstyles can also increase apparent height.
Tall	Sports coats and contrasting pants will help break up the appearance of extreme height. Tight-fitting pants and jackets will make you seem even taller.	Wear outfits that break in the middle and have top and bottom contrasting colors. Use slim heels. Hats and hairdos should not add inches.
Overweight	Be well-tailored. Don't let clothes show overweight areas noticeably. Double-breasted jackets tend to give a thinning appearance. Black and navy are slimming colors.	Avoid large prints and fabrics like jersey that cling and reveal bulges. Long earrings are a good idea—they tend to lengthen the neck. Black and navy are good colors.
Thin	You can wear all fabrics, even the heavy ones, without fear of looking too bulky. If your arms are too thin, wear long sleeves.	You can wear almost all clothes. If certain features are too prominent, deemphasize them. For example, a long neck can be hidden with a scarf, turtleneck, or high collar. Avoid a low neckline. Nubby materials will give added weight.
Average	Emphasize your good features, minimize your poorer features. You have a wide range of styles to choose from.	Same. Do not wear a mini skirt if you have heavy legs. Fit the fashion to your body type.

new wardrobe, take an inventory of what you already have and plan to fill in the gaps.

Every wardrobe should have balance. Most of us have weaknesses for certain types of clothing or accessories. If you do, then some self-discipline is in order. Don't overstock one segment of your wardrobe at the expense of other segments.

Plan your wardrobe according to your anticipated lifestyle. Give priority to business clothes, but don't ignore the dress-up or casual parts of your life. In developing your wardrobe, here are some things to think about:

PUTTING TOGETHER A WARDROBE

- Know your taste in clothes. Take time to think about the kinds of clothing left hanging in the closet and the kinds you're always wearing. Clothes that never get out of the closet are bad purchases. When you recognize what they are, and why, you'll save yourself a lot of money by not making the same mistakes again.
- Don't skimp on important items, such as a coat or shoes, or anything you wear a lot. In the long run, you'll save if you buy quality.
- Whenever possible, buy fabrics that can be worn through all the seasons. This will reduce the need for buying a new wardrobe several times a year. Synthetic blends, corduroys, and light knits are some of the excellent all-year-round fabrics.
- If you've bought several very satisfactory items from one store, manufacturer, or designer, look for more from the same source.
- Be aware of the cost of upkeep of anything you intend to buy. For example, suede and down-filled products are expensive to have cleaned.
- Don't buy something that needs extensive alteration, especially a sale item that really isn't your size. Too much altering changes the proportion of clothes and they'll never look right.
- Buy one or two pairs of quality, well-fitting slacks or skirts in basic styles and colors. Then buy jackets and shirts or blouses (both dressy and casual) to go with them. Even though you keep wearing the same pants or skirts, you'll look different because of the varying combinations.
- Shop in stores that have a good return or exchange policy in case you buy defective merchandise.

(list continued on next page)

CLOTHING

PUTTING TOGETHER A WARDROBE

- Check sales for out-of-season bargains. Most stores have good sales at the end of the season to make room for the next season's merchandise. But don't buy what you don't really need.
- There are many discount stores that sell department-store brands for 20% or 30% less. Shop these stores first. Also, if there are clothing manufacturers in your area, they may have outlets where they sell their merchandise at a discount. But don't get confused by the word outlet. If there's no factory nearby, chances are you'll be paying retail prices.
- Spend the time and/or money to keep clothes and shoes in good repair. Don't wait too long to have the repairs done. The damage may become irreparable.

If new clothes are beyond your economic reach, try visiting thrift shops and the re-sale stores run by many charitable organizations. They can be a bargain-hunter's paradise. Sometimes, great finds also come from flea markets and garage sales.

Clothing Labels

Today, with the great number of textiles and materials being used in the fabrication of garments, it's often difficult for a consumer to know exactly what fibers or combination of fibers he or she is buying.

The U.S. Government has labeling regulations to help consumers judge the quality of clothing. Here is some of the information that must appear in a conspicuous place in most garments:

CLOTHING LABELS TO HELP CONSUMERS

- Every garment must have a label with the name or code number of the manufacturer.
- If different kinds of fibers are used in a garment, the label must tell the percentages (in order of predominance by weight) and generic names of all fibers present (if these fibers amount to 5% or more of the total). This prevents false advertising or labeling that would lead consumers to believe the garment is made of expensive material when, in fact, the expensive fibers are only a small percentage of the blend.
- There is specific labeling required to identify wool as virgin, reprocessed, or reused. Wool is fiber from the fleece of a sheep or lamb or the hair of Angora or Kashmir (Cashmere) goat (and may include the so-called specialty fibers from the hair of alpaca, camel, llama, or vicuna) which has never been reclaimed from any woven or felted product. Virgin or new wool means wool fiber that has never been used or made into any product before. Reprocessed wool refers to wool fibers that have never been woven or felted into a wool product used by a consumer. Reused wool means fiber reclaimed from woolen products that have been used by a consumer.
- Much consumer confusion is caused by the approximately 700 trade names for man-made fibers. To clarify matters, the Federal Trade Commission has grouped these fibers into generic groups. This makes it easier to know what kinds of fabric you are buying. The generic groups include: acetate, acrylic, anidex, azlon, glass, metallic, modacrylic, nylon, nytril, olefin, polyester, rayon, rubber, saran, spandex, vinal, and vinyon. A generic name cannot be used if the fiber is less than 5% of the total fabric. Exceptions are made when the fiber has functional significance. For example, manufacturers may state on the label: "4% spandex for elasticity."

(list continued on next page)

CLOTHING LABELS TO HELP CONSUMERS

- Fur labels must list: 1) the true English name of the animal producing the fur; 2) the country of origin if the fur is imported; 3) whether the fur is dyed, bleached, artificially colored, or its natural color; 4) whether the fur is composed of paws, bellies, scrap pieces, or waste furs; and 5) the name or registered identification number of the manufacturer or distributor.
- Care labels required by the Federal Trade Commission indicate how to wash, bleach, dry, iron, or dry clean various garments. They must be placed in all clothing products except some hosiery products, headwear, handwear, footwear, disposable items, washable garments retailing for $3 or less, fur and leather items, purely decorative or ornamental items, remnants cut and shipped by the manufacturer, and see-through or other items whose appearance would be substantially impaired by a label (such as a chiffon scarf). Regard care labels cautiously, because they are frequently too conservative or incorrect. If you've followed the advice of a care label and damage to the garment resulted, bring the item back to the store where it was purchased.

CARING FOR YOUR CLOTHES

Clothes will last much longer if you hang them up as soon as you remove them. Wear a robe or old clothes while you work or lounge around the house. Don't cram clothes into a closet, and avoid hanging clothes on hooks unless the garments have special loops. Invest in extra hangers if necessary.

Wash or dry clean clothes only when necessary. Repeated cleanings can weaken fabrics. Different kinds of fibers require different treatments. Use the following chart as a guide.

FIBER CARE CHART
Reprinted from The Butterick Fabric Handbook.

Fiber	General Care	Special Instructions
acetate	Usually dry clean. If labeled for washing, wash by hand in warm water and mild suds. Don't wring or twist, don't soak colored fabrics. Press while slightly damp on wrong side with cool iron or use a press cloth on the right side.	Keep away from acetone (nail polish remover, for example). It dissolves acetate.
acrylic	Most items should be washed in warm water by hand. Squeeze out water, don't wring. Smooth item and dry on hanger. If labeled for machine washing, use warm water, machine dry at low, and remove from dryer as soon as tumbling cycle is over.	Dry knitted items flat (they'll stretch otherwise). Static electricity build-up can be reduced by using fabric softener in every four or five washings, whether by hand or machine (not more often—it tends to dull clothes).
anidex	May be washed or dry cleaned depending on fibers used with it. May be tumbled or drip dried. Use a moderate heat setting if ironing is necessary.	This elastic man-made fiber (unlike spandex) is not damaged by chlorine bleach.
cotton	Most 100% cottons can be washed by machine at the regular cycle with hot water, and dried at the regular setting. Use chlorine bleach only on whites and colored fabrics that you have tested for color retention. High temperature iron setting may be used. Wash cotton knits by hand to avoid excessive shrinkage.	Don't assume that all cotton fabrics are colorfast. Check the label or test a small portion; if the color runs, have the item dry cleaned.

(chart continued on next page)

CLOTHING

FIBER CARE CHART
Reprinted from The Butterick Fabric Handbook.

Fiber	*General Care*	*Special Instructions*
glass fibers	Wash only by hand and hang to dry while wet.	Be careful in washing—slivers of glass can injure hands.
linen	Machine wash in hot water, dry at regular cycle. Dark colors should be washed in water of a lower temperature to keep them from fading. Dry cleaning is especially satisfactory for color and shape retention of linens.	Do not bleach colored linens.
modacrylic	Pile garments (fake furs, for instance) should be dry cleaned or cleaned commercially by the fur method. Some items are washable. Machine wash in warm water, use low setting of dryer and remove items promptly.	A fabric softener will reduce static electricity in the washable items. Use lowest possible setting when ironing is necessary; modacrylic is extremely sensitive to heat.
nylon	Most items can be machine washed in warm water and tumble dried at low setting. Remove from dryer promptly to avoid heat-set wrinkles. If ironing is desired, use only a warm iron. Nylon tends to pick up colors from other fabrics if not washed separately. Sponge upholstery and rugs or use special cleaners for these items.	Static electricity can be reduced by the use of fabric softener in every four or five washings.
olefin	Machine wash in lukewarm water, machine dry only at lowest setting. Remove from dryer as soon as tumbling stops. Do not dry in a commercial or laundromat type gas-fired dryer. In blends, use lowest possible setting	Notice cautions on temperature for drying and ironing.

(chart continued on next page)

FIBER CARE CHART
Reprinted from The Butterick Fabric Handbook.

Fiber	General Care	Special Instructions
	when ironing. Never iron 100% olefin. Stains on rugs, carpets, and upholstery can be sponged clean.	
polyester	Machine washing at a warm setting with drying at a low temperature is recommended for polyester. Remove items from the dryer promptly to avoid heat-set wrinkles. Iron with a moderately warm iron. Some white polyesters pick up color from other fabrics; wash separately if this would be objectionable. Polyester fabrics can be dry cleaned but watch prints—some color substances often used on printed polyesters are injured by dry cleaning.	Avoid over-drying of polyester and especially of polyester knits—it will give the effect of shrinkage. Notice caution on dry cleaning of polyesters.
rayon	Dry cleaning is definitely safest for rayon; however, if washing, wash by hand in lukewarm water. Do not wring or twist, and don't use chlorine bleach as some finishes on rayon are chlorine retentive, which leads to yellowing and loss of strength. Smooth the item, hang on hanger to dry, press while still damp on the wrong side with a moderate iron or use a pressing cloth on the right side.	Notice caution on the use of chlorine bleach.
saran	Saran fibers are usually found domestically only on garden furniture; sponge or hose clean.	

(chart continued on next page)

CLOTHING 99

FIBER CARE CHART
Reprinted from The Butterick Fabric Handbook.

Fiber	General Care	Special Instructions
silk	Dry cleaning is best for silk, although some silks can be hand washed (only if so labeled). Squeeze suds through fabric; do not wring or twist. Iron on the wrong side. To avoid water spotting (marks made by drops of water) do not use steam when pressing silk. Iron at medium temperature.	Never use chlorine bleach on silk.
spandex	Wash by hand or machine in lukewarm water, drip dry or dry at low temperature by machine.	Do not use chlorine bleach: spandex is chlorine-retentive and will yellow and lose strength. Avoid ironing. If ironing is essential, iron rapidly at the lowest possible temperature setting. Spandex slowly disintegrates from heat.
triacetate	Machine wash and dry at normal hot settings, except pleated items, which should be hand washed. A high iron temperature may be used.	Keep away from acetone—see caution for acetate.
vinyon	Sponge vinyon clean.	
wool	Woven woolens should be dry cleaned, except for those labeled "washable." Follow care instructions on such woolens exactly. Machine-made knitted woolens should also be dry cleaned, unless labeled "washable," in which case follow label instructions. The dry cleaner should be told these fabrics are woolens to ensure that the proper technique is used in cleaning and drying. Hand wash socks, mittens, and hand-knit items in lukewarm or cold water using special soap for wool.	Never use chlorine bleach on wool. Dry knits flat to avoid stretching. To iron, always keep a damp cloth between the fabric and the iron.

Doing Your Laundry

Laundromats and commercial machines in apartment houses can be hard on clothes. Very often they do not have temperature or cycle control features to use with items that need special care. You'll have to experiment with these machines to find the exact procedures for getting the best results. If you have your own machines, you'll have an easier time controlling the quality of your wash.

No matter whose machines you use, there are steps for doing the laundry that are necessary for good results.

Avoid the temptation to throw all of your clothes into the washer or dryer at one time. Overloading these machines will result in a poor-quality wash and can damage the machines as well.

Special Care Items

Down-filled vests, coats, or comforters should never be placed in the washing machine. These need to be specially handled by a competent dry cleaner.

Leather also needs special attention. There are two types of leather that you should be aware of, because they require different cleaning techniques. The first is smooth leather (shiny or matte finish) and the second is suede (or suede-looking leathers such as chamois, buckskin, and shearling).

To remove surface dirt from smooth leather, wipe it with a damp cloth dipped in mild soap and water, pat dry, dust lightly with baby powder, and then rub with a clean cloth.

For suede, or suede-like leather, rub against the grain with a sponge or brush (plastic or nylon) to raise the nap. For major stains such as grease, ink, or sugar, take the garment to a dry cleaner who specializes in leather. Before you store a suede item, have it professionally cleaned and hang it on a contoured or padded hanger to keep the suede shoulder line in shape. Drape a cloth across the shoulders so that surface dust won't darken the color. Empty all leather and suede pockets to

STEPS FOR DOING THE LAUNDRY

1. Separate your machine washables from the clothes that require hand washing or dry cleaning.
2. Divide the rest of your wash into piles of "delicates," "whites," "dark colors that may run," "towels and other heavy-duty items," and "all others." Keep apart any items that are severely stained.
3. Soak the stained items in a commercial pre-soak product according to package directions.
4. Select one pile of your pre-sorted clothes and select the proper machine cycles. Before adding the clothes, turn on the machine and add detergent while the water is running. Don't use more than you need. Now put in the clothes. If you're unsure whether an item is colorfast, dissolve one teaspoon of detergent in a cup of hot water and put a few drops of this hot solution on a seam or another hidden area of the garment. Let it sit for 5 minutes, then rinse the area and check for any color change.
5. Add fabric softener and bleaches to the wash load at the appropriate point in the cycle. You can add them with the detergent if your machine is equipped with special dispensers. Be sure to read the directions before using these products. Permanent damage to your clothes can result if you're not careful.
6. Remove clothes from the machine as soon as the unit shuts off.
7. Hang up "delicates" to dry.
8. If you are using a machine dryer, select the proper cycles before you load in the clothes. Articles containing rubber, plastic, or vinyl should never be placed in the dryer.
9. Remove clothes as soon as they are dry. Overdrying causes wrinkling.
10. Repeat this procedure for each pile of your wash until the whole job is finished.

prevent sags or bulges. Don't use airtight garment bags. They can discolor leather and suede.

To press leather, use a rayon or low setting on your iron. Do not use steam and never place the iron directly on the garment. Use a press cloth of heavy wrapping paper and work the iron lightly up and down the surface.

Leather boots are made from animal skin and require cleaning and moisturizing. For delicate leathers such as kidskin, a neutral cream is a good cleaning-moisturizing agent. Saddle soap works best on heavy leathers, but it can dull the finish and even crack the surface on delicate leathers. Suede boots or shoes need brushing with very fine sandpaper or a dry sponge.

Clean vinyl and cloth boots or shoes by wiping them with a sponge dampened in non-detergent soap. To repel stains, spray with a silicone spray. Clear nail polish will prevent tarnish or chips on metal buttons or buckles.

When storing shoes or boots for the summer, stuff them with newspaper or cardboard to keep them in shape. Make sure boots are covered.

Removing Stains

In day-to-day living, accidents happen and stains result. Often they require the services of a professional cleaner. But with a little acquired skill and a touch of elbow grease, you can handle many of them yourself.

For best results, you should always deal with stains at once. If a stain is of unknown origin but seems non-greasy, soak it in cold water, then wash it in warm suds. If the stain seems greasy, sponge with carbon tetrachloride or a similar dry cleaning solvent, then wash.

Always try any chemicals used in stain removal on the inside of a hem or in another inconspicuous place. If the results aren't satisfactory, don't go any further.

The "Stain Removal Chart" on the next page should help you with problem stains.

STAIN REMOVAL CHART

Reprinted from The Butterick Fabric Handbook.

Stain	Removal Method
ballpoint pen ink	Ballpoint pen ink comes out quite easily when sponged with rubbing alcohol. On a washable fabric, any stain that remains should be rubbed with soap or a detergent and then the fabric should be washed. The same method should be used on non-washable items, followed by sponging with a mild detergent solution of 1 teaspoon detergent to 1 cup of water.
blood	Washable fabrics should be soaked in cold water immediately. If they do not respond to cold water, an enzyme pre-soak (when available) should be used. The fabrics should then be washed in the usual way. Non-washable items should be sponged with cold water followed by a mild detergent solution (1 teaspoon detergent to 1 cup of water). If the detergent solution doesn't work, try a solution of 1 tablespoon ammonia in a cup of water—and if that changes the color of the item, follow it up by sponging with ¼ cup white vinegar in 1 cup of water to bring back the original color. Test both the ammonia solution and the vinegar solution in some inconspicuous spot before using on the stain.
candle wax	Follow instructions for chewing gum, below.
chewing gum	Chewing gum can be removed from most fabrics if it is first hardened by rubbing it with an ice cube and then scraped off with a blunt knife or your fingernail. This takes time and patience but it does work. In desperate cases, you can try sponging the gum with a nonflammable cleaning fluid, but this can spread the stain.
coffee, tea	Simple washing will usually remove coffee and tea stains on washable fabrics. On non-washable fabrics, sponge with cold water first, then try a mild detergent solution of 1 teaspoon of detergent to 1 cup of water.

(chart continues on next page)

STAIN REMOVAL CHART

Reprinted from The Butterick Fabric Handbook.

Stain	Removal Method
cream, milk	Washing will remove cream and milk from washable fabrics. On non-washable fabrics, start by wiping with a damp sponge. If that fails, shake cornstarch or white talcum powder onto the stain, allow to dry thoroughly, then use a brush or vacuum to remove the residue.
greasy stains, including lipstick, tar	Start by following the ice-cube method given for chewing gum, then use lighter fluid to remove any remaining stain on both washable and non-washable fabrics.
nail polish	Nail polish remover will remove nail polish from most fabrics, but NEVER use it on acetate or triacetate. On these fabrics, try to scrape the polish off with a blunt knife or fingernail.
paint (oil based)	See instructions for nail polish, above.
paint (water based)	If the paint is still wet, sponge with water, trying not to spread the stain further. If the paint is dry, nothing (including dry cleaning) will get it out, but you may be able to scrape some off the surface with a blunt knife or your fingernail.
perspiration	Certain man-made fibers seem to hold perspiration odors longer than other fabrics; although a stain will come out with washing, the odor may not. Rub the area of the odor with a deodorant soap before washing.
urine, vomit, mucus	Soak washable fabrics in an enzyme pre-soak (if possible), then wash using a suitable bleach (chlorine or oxygen type). On non-washable items, such as rugs, sponge first with mild detergent solution (1 teaspoon of detergent to a cup of water) and rinse. If that doesn't work, try white vinegar solution—¼ cup of white vinegar to 1 cup of water. If this solution changes the color, try to neutralize it with an ammonia solution of 1 tablespoon of ammonia to 1 cup of water. Test both the ammonia solution and the vinegar solution in an inconspicuous spot before using either on the stain.

CLOTHING

Basic Clothing Repairs

Sewing really isn't difficult. It just takes patience and practice. Here are a few quick tips that may save your day, or at least help you cope with an emergency that may befall you before an important event:

Sewing on Buttons, Snaps, and Hooks and Eyes Probably the toughest part is finding just where to put the closer. If there's some left-over thread in the fabric, your job is easy—just clean out the old thread and sew the new closer on at that spot. If that's not possible, you'll have to mark the spot with pins. First close the garment so it fits properly. Then, for buttons, put a pin through the buttonhole and into the fabric underneath. For snaps and hooks and eyes, first put a pin at the proper spot on the underside of the overlapping fabric, then close the garment, turn the flap back gently to find the pin, and put another pin at the appropriate spot in the fabric beneath.

Since thread for sewing on these closers must withstand wear, use buttonhole twist, button and carpet thread, heavy-duty thread, or a double strand of cotton thread coated with beeswax. Use an 18″ length to avoid tangles.

The names of buttons correspond to the way they are attached to a garment. There are sew-through buttons, shank buttons, and reinforced buttons.

Sew-through buttons (buttons with two or four holes) work better if you add a shank or stem of thread as you sew them on. The thread shank prevents the fabric around the closure from being distorted, and it should be as long as the garment is thick at the buttonhole, plus a scant ⅛″ for movement. Form the shank by putting a small object such as a toothpick or bobby pin over the button between the holes; sew over the object when you attach the button. When the button is secure, remove the object and wind the thread tightly under the button to form the shank. Securely fasten the thread to the shank. If you are using sew-through buttons for trim, a thread shank is unnecessary.

Shank buttons (those with a built-in shank) are attached with small stitches sewn through the hole in the shank (sometimes it's a loop). Align the shank with the buttonhole so that the threads will be parallel to the opening edge. An additional thread shank may be needed for very thick fabric.

Reinforced buttons are used for coats, suits, or delicate fabrics. For coats, place a small, flat button on the inside of the garment directly under the outer button, and sew from one to the other, making thread shanks as needed. For delicate fabrics, substitute a small, folded, square of ribbon seam binding for the inner button. At neck or wrist openings, or anyplace where the inner surface can show, place the square of binding between the garment and the inner-facing.

Snaps and hooks and eyes make quick, easy closures. When positioning a snap, remember that the ball section of the snap (the part with the protruding knob) should be sewn to the overlapping garment section. The socket section (the one with the indentation) is applied to the underlapping section. Sew the snap sections in place with small, close stitches, taking four or five stitches in each hole. Secure the thread tightly.

Hooks will withstand the strain of body movement and give a smooth finish. Sew the hook to the overlapping section of the garment and attach the eye or loop directly beneath the hook on the underlapping garment section. Secure with tiny stitches, as described above for snaps.

Hems

Hemming a garment sounds more difficult than it really is. Hems can be sewn with hemming stitches, catchstitches, or blindstitches.

Hemming stitch is used for hems that are finished with seam binding. Take a tiny stitch in the garment, then bring the needle diagonally through the seam binding or hem edge. Do all the stitches in this manner, spacing them about ¼" apart.

BASIC WARDROBE REPAIRS

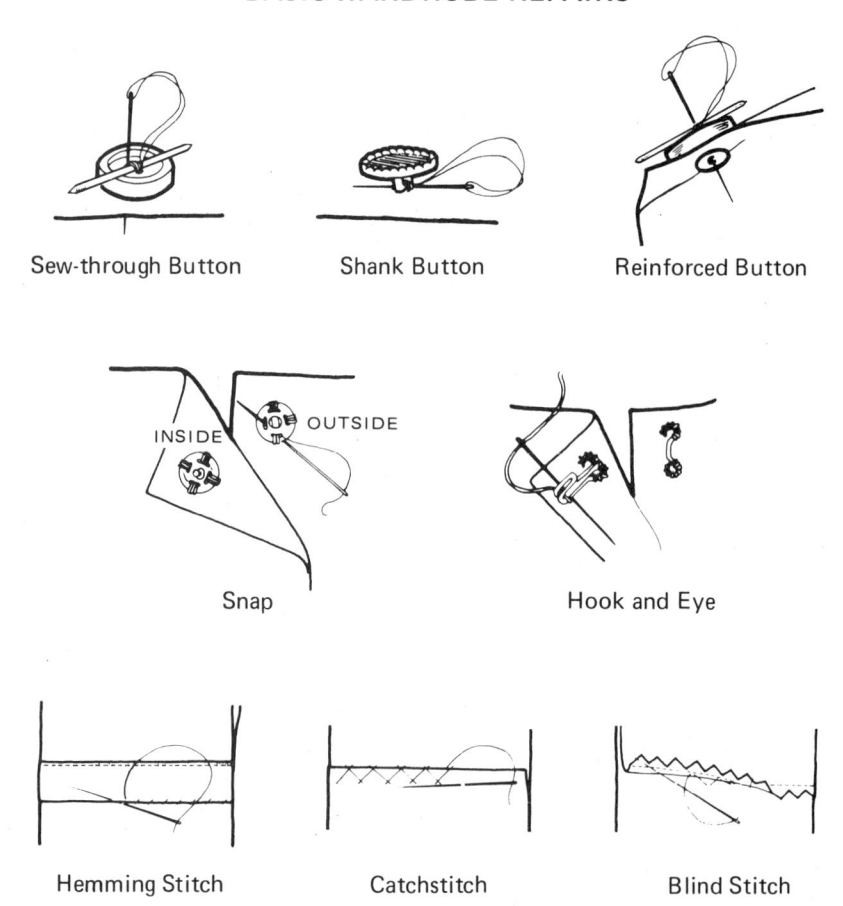

Sew-through Button   Shank Button   Reinforced Button

Snap   Hook and Eye

Hemming Stitch   Catchstitch   Blind Stitch

Catchstitch is used to hem stretchy fabrics, since it's good for holding two layers of fabric in place flexibly. Work from left to right. Start by taking a small horizontal stitch from right to left in the upper layer of fabric. Then, just below the edge of the upper layer, take an identical small stitch in the underlayer, but somewhat to the right of the other stitch. Move the needle up and to the right, and make another small stitch in the upper layer, and so on. Finish sewing the hem in this loose zigzag manner.

Blindstitch is used when you don't want the stitches to be visible on either side of the garment. First take a small horizontal stitch through one thread of the garment. Then pick up a thread of the hem, diagonally above the previous stitch. Work in a zigzag manner. Don't pull the stitches too tight. Every 4 or 5 inches, stretch the blindstitched area and take a few extra stitches in the hem allowance (not the garment) for a more durable, rip-proof hem.

These are just quick pointers on home-sewing. There are books and magazines that can tell you more about the subject. If you're all thumbs, you could take your alterations to a professional seamstress or tailor.

Now that you're aware of what's involved in providing shelter, food, and clothing, let's examine how the independent life can be financed.

4 MONEY

Finding a Job

Interviewing

Managing Your Money

Banking: The Basics

Credit

Insurance

Investments

Taxes

Legalities

FINDING A JOB

Without a job your road to independence will be rocky, if not impassable. Whether you're setting out for the first time, taking a new direction, or returning after an absence, you need to consider what your real interests are and what you're especially qualified to do.

A career should never be chosen for you. When people attempt to tell you what to do, it's usually more a matter of what will make *them* happy. That doesn't mean you shouldn't let others guide you. Family, friends, teachers, and professional career counselors may give you insights as to your capabilities and make you aware of opportunities you never knew existed.

A career choice doesn't have to be an everlasting commitment. Attempt what really appeals to you. If it doesn't work, make a change before it's too late. Procrastination, fear of failure, or the weight of obligations trap many people in careers that are totally unfulfilling. Financial security has a powerful hold, but if you're uncomfortable or bored in a job, you probably won't perform at your best. It's better to take a chance at a different job if it helps you preserve your inner peace.

Temper your career choice with a degree of practicality. Is your ambition really attainable? Check out the personal and educational qualifications for your career choice, the number of openings versus the number of applicants, and the time it may take you to reach a reasonable level of success.

Research your choice by visiting your local library; talking to friends, family, teachers, and counselors; and by interviewing people who hold the job you think you want. Then evaluate yourself and the career in light of your findings. Make sure your choice of job will lead to the kind of life you would like to have.

How to Find a Job

Finding a job is in some ways similar to finding a place to live. The very best availabilities are made known by word-of-mouth. The quickest route to a job is by a personal referral to the person who is doing the hiring, so let others know what kind of work you are seeking. You never know whose friend or relative is looking for an employee with your qualifications.

If nothing comes along the "grapevine," check the "employee wanted" section of your local newspaper. Jobs are usually listed by type of work. Scan the entire section for the job titles that describe the kind of work you want. Be wary of jobs that sound too good to be true—they usually are!

Some newspaper ads are placed by employment agencies. If you answer one of these ads, you may have to pay an agency fee if you accept a job. Many employment agencies receive a month's salary or 10% of your yearly pay, or more for placing you in a position. This fee may be paid by your employer (this is called a "fee paid" job). If it isn't, you will have to pay the fee personally. Be sure you understand your obligations before accepting a position through an employment agency.

Other sources of job opening information include placement offices at the school from which you have graduated, professional organizations for the career you are considering, and bulletin boards in public buildings (such as schools and libraries) or in commercial establishments (such as supermarkets).

If you have your eye on a job in a particular company, don't be bashful about writing to or visiting its personnel office (or the boss if the company is small). You may get the job you really want by demonstrating your eagerness to work for the particular company and by convincing them that you're really qualified.

When you write to a company, make sure your letter is attractive and free of errors. Be businesslike. Make your job inquiry brief, yet convince them to call you for an interview. Remember to include your address and telephone number in your letter.

Some businesses require that you send a resumé with your inquiry letter. A resumé is a brief (one page is fine) personal history. It should contain your name, address, telephone number, educational background, and previous business experience.

There are many books available that contain step-by-step instructions for writing resumés. Here is a sample of one format; there are many others that are acceptable.

SAMPLE RESUMÉ

JANE DOE
56 Elm Street
Somerset, New York 13579
(212) 135-7911

CAREER OBJECTIVE:	A position as an assistant buyer in a department store or buying office with opportunities for advancement.
EDUCATION:	B.A., Fashion Merchandising New York University June, 1980 Diploma, June, 1976 Somerset High School Somerset, New York 13579
WORK EXPERIENCE:	
Spring, 1980	Manley's Department Store Fifth Avenue New York, New York 12468 Position: Student Intern Worked in two-week modules in the following departments within the store: sales, advertising, personnel, and customer relations. Spent eight weeks of the internship assisting a Junior sportswear buyer with merchandise selection, display, stock work, inventory control, and routine clerical work.
1976–1980	Grandee's Department Store Main Street Somerset, New York 13579 Position: Assistant Floor Manager Was promoted to this position in the Junior dress department after working for two years as a salesperson in Misses dresses. Responsibilities included: handling customer returns and complaints, scheduling departmental employees, authorizing special transactions, and inventory control.
1974–1976	Somerset Variety Store Main Street Somerset, New York 13579 Position: Stock Clerk and Relief Cashier Responsible for maintaining appearance of stock. Handled customer transactions in absence of cashier.
HONORS:	Dean's List, New York University Elected to Teen Advisory Board, Fashion Magazine, 1978.

REFERENCES AVAILABLE UPON REQUEST

INTERVIEWING

Once a prospective employer becomes interested in you, he or she will probably make an appointment to meet you.

Your appearance at the interview is very important. Dress naturally in attractive, appropriate clothing. Avoid jeans, chewing gum, heavy make-up, and too much perfume or jewelry.

Arrive a few minutes early for your interview. You may have to submit your resumé or fill in a job application (or both).

Job applications are your introduction to a prospective employer. Fill them out neatly and follow the directions exactly. Make yourself as appealing as possible, but never lie. Job applications occasionally include questions about your reason for wanting the job, and your overall career goals. Do some thinking about those questions *before* the interview.

When you meet the interviewer, shake his or her hand firmly. Answer all questions directly and make as much eye contact as is comfortable for you. Listen to what the interviewer has to say. Remember, the interviewer knows the company—and its needs—better than you do. Don't attempt to do all the talking or to tell too much.

When the interview is over and you have returned home, immediately write a letter to the interviewer thanking him or her for taking the time to see you. Be persistent in following up the interview if you're interested in the job, but don't be a pest.

If you accept the job, make sure you understand what your job entails, when you will begin working, and what salary and benefits you will receive. If you and your employer start off in a misunderstanding, neither of you will be satisfied later.

MANAGING YOUR MONEY

Once you begin working and earning a salary, you'll have to think about managing your money. Of great concern to everyone these days is the shrinking purchasing power of the dollar. How can you stretch your pay and thereby get the most value for your money?

A budget is of primary importance (see page 4). Knowing what your monthly obligations are will guide you in determining the amount you have left over for savings, for unforeseen emergencies, and for fun.

According to studies done by First National City Bank (Consumer Views, Vol. V, No. 8), the following are valuable tips for stretching your dollars:

STRETCHING YOUR DOLLAR

1. **Set Priorities.** Before buying anything, make a distinction between what's nice and what's necessary. This is strictly a personal evaluation. Whereas a car might be nice for someone who will use it to get away on weekends, it might be absolutely essential to another person who will use it to make business calls.

    Furthermore, there are different price levels to consider. Some products are fancier or more complex than others. If you are shopping for a television set, you must decide on color versus black and white, on a 16" screen versus a 19" screen. In the end, your ultimate decision should be based on the value of the product in terms of the importance it will play in your life. If you make objective decisions, you will more than likely live within your financial level and have better command of your income.
2. **Control Your Cash.** If you're not careful, cash has a way of disappearing. How often have you asked yourself, "Where did it all go?" Well, for openers, how about transportation, laundry, lunch, tips, entertainment, snacks, gifts, and so forth?

(tips continued on next page)

STRETCHING YOUR DOLLAR

To know where your cash went and to prevent it from going where it shouldn't, you must keep track of out-of-pocket expenditures regularly—at least once a day. If there are large discrepancies between what you think you spent and what's actually left, it's a sign that you're not as attentive to your expenditures as you should be. Good times to check your cash are just after lunch and/or in the evening when the day's spending is over.

3. **Know Your Billing Cycles.** Be aware of how billing cycles work. Take, for example, routine responsibilities such as dental check-ups. Suppose your dentist regularly bills on the first of the month. Schedule your appointment for the third of the month so you won't get a bill for at least three weeks.
4. **Bargain Hunt.** This is a foolproof way to get more value for your money. Be diligent, buy out of season, and use discount stores and factory outlets. Keep an eye out for warehouse and clearance sales.

Be sure to comparison shop. You can do this by actually visiting stores, or you can assemble a file of newspaper ads, especially on significantly priced items (TV, stereo, furniture). Always be prepared for traditional sale periods.

January: The big month for inventory clearances. Christmas cards, wrappings, decorations on sale; also the month for White Sales on towels and bedding.

February: Washington and Lincoln's Birthday storewide sales.

March and April: After-Easter storewide sales.

May: Memorial Day storewide sales.

July: Fourth of July storewide sales. Summer fashion clearances begin.

August: Another month for White Sales. A good time to start shopping for bargains in cars.

September: Labor Day specials. Watch for sales on tires and car clearances.

October: Columbus Day storewide sales.

November: Election Day and Veterans' Day storewide sales.

December: After-Christmas clearances.

(tips continued on next page)

STRETCHING YOUR DOLLAR

5. **Curb Impulse Buying.** Controlling impulse spending is a "must." It's a good idea to hold off on the impulse to buy for a couple of days. Often the desire fades.

    You can also control impulse spending by setting a weekly limit for out-of-pocket expenditures. Let's say it's $5 per weekday or a total of $25 per work week. You should furnish yourself with five $5 bills at the beginning of the week. Larger or smaller bills could cause confusion. On Wednesday morning you should wake up with three $5 bills. If you have less, you have spent too much on Monday and Tuesday and should plan on cutbacks for the rest of the week. By not having more cash on hand, you cannot spend on impulse.

6. **Know How Much to Tip.** Psychologists have often said that overtipping is a sign of insecurity. It's also one of the fastest ways of putting money that should be in your pocket into someone else's pocket. On the other hand, undertipping is an insulting way to short-change good service. It's better to strike a happy medium, one that is fair to everyone, including yourself.

    Waiters and Waitresses: 15% of the bill in better restaurants, 20% in exceptional ones. At a counter 10%–15% is considered adequate at breakfast or lunch, 15%–20% at dinner. Cocktail waiters or waitresses should get 15% (minimum 50 cents per person). Wine stewards, one dollar per bottle.

    Bartender: 15% if you're sitting at the bar, nothing if you're sitting at a table and you're served by someone else.

    Taxi Driver: 25 cents minimum, usually 20% of the bill.

    Airport Porter: 50 cents to a dollar per bag, depending on whether he loads it into the taxi or car himself, or hands it to someone else at the curb.

    Red Cap (in bus terminals): There is usually a fixed cost per bag and the Red Cap is tipped an additional amount, usually 50 cents.

    Bellhop: 50 cents to a dollar per bag.

(tips continued on next page)

STRETCHING YOUR DOLLAR

Chambermaid: Nothing if your stay is very short. A dollar or two per night if you stay longer, and more if she or he performs extra services.

Hotel or Apartment Door Guard: 50 cents to a dollar if he or she hails a cab; otherwise nothing.

Ladies Room/Mens Room Attendant: 25 cents optional unless they perform a service.

Hat Check Attendant: 50 cents per person. Sometimes a set fee.

Christmas Tipping: In many cities, it is customary to give a Christmas tip to those who have rendered services all year long. The people you might consider for such a gratuity include your building superintendent; the door guard; elevator operator; hairdresser; regular babysitter; those who deliver the milk, newspaper, and mail; garage attendant; and cleaning help. As you can see, the list can get quite lengthy—and expensive. Here's a rule of thumb—a Christmas tip, from $2 to $10, should be given only to those who have rendered exceptional service during the year.

BANKING: THE BASICS

What is a Bank?

Commercial banks are nongovernment financial institutions that provide checking accounts, savings accounts, various consumer loans (such as auto, home improvement, and education), and safe-deposit facilities. They sell and redeem U.S. Savings Bonds; prepare cash payrolls for local businesses; offer mortgages on residential and commercial property; offer Christmas and other club savings accounts; issue bank credit cards, travelers checks, and bank money orders; and, in many instances, provide trust services.

Banks make a profit from interest on loans and from investments the bank makes in government and private securities. Bank deposits are used to make loans and investments, and to pay bank operating expenses such as salaries. Since commercial banks are corporations and are owned by stockholders, they return a portion of profits to shareholders in the form of dividends.

Savings banks, or savings and loan banks, are formed essentially to provide mortgage loans; they also offer savings accounts. However, by its very nature, a savings bank does not offer the range of services provided by a commercial bank.

Checking Accounts

One way to become a bank's customer is to open a checking account. A checking account is not only a convenient method of paying bills, it also eliminates the need to have large sums of cash on hand. It saves the expense of obtaining money orders to pay routine bills and allows you to pay bills by mail rather than taking the time and spending the money for transportation, and possibly parking, to pay bills with cash in person.

You can open a special checking account or a regular checking account. Special checking does not require that a minimum balance be kept in the account. However, you pay for each check you write and you incur a monthly maintenance fee. A regular checking account is designed for people who can keep a minimum balance (usually $500 or more) in the account. If you maintain or exceed the minimum each month, there is no maintenance charge. If you fall short, then you pay fees according to your bank's fee schedule. Some specialized regular checking accounts are available that pay interest on your checkbook balances.

The choice of special or regular checking must be based on your financial position. If you can't afford to keep a steady minimum balance, then it's better to pay the fees that come with a special checking account.

The following questions frequently come up concerning checking accounts.

FREQUENTLY ASKED QUESTIONS ABOUT CHECKS

Q. If the amount of a check shown in figures is different from the amount written out, does the bank refuse to pay the check?

A. No. The bank regards the amount written out as the correct figure. If you realize after a check has left your hands that it contains an error, call your bank and stop payment.

Q. Is a check valid if it is dated on a Sunday or holiday?

A. Yes. It's not true that checks can only be dated on days when banks are open. However, a check over six months old may be rejected. In January and February it is especially important to date your checks with the correct year.

Q. Why do I have to balance the bank statement with my check book? Doesn't the bank keep my account straight?

A. The bank keeps a running daily record of the status of your account. However, the bank doesn't know what checks you have written until they are presented for payment. To avoid writing a check in an amount larger than your account balance, you must keep accurate records. If your bank statement seems to indicate a discrepancy, check it promptly and notify your bank.

Q. How and when should you stop payment on a check?

A. If you write a check for an incorrect amount or wish to revoke a check written to a person or company, you may instruct your bank to refuse payment on it. To do this, call or visit your bank immediately with the check number and the payee's name and amount. If the check has not already been paid, the bank will issue a stop payment order, indicating that the check should not be paid when presented. In the meantime you will receive a form to sign and return. This will verify your stop payment request. There is a charge for this service. Ask your bank for the exact amount at the outset.

Q. How long does a stop payment continue in effect?

A. It will remain in effect for six months. If the check hasn't been presented for payment during that time, you may renew the stop payment order.

Savings Accounts

Savings accounts can be opened at either commercial or savings banks. There are minor variations offered by banks. For instance, some banks pay higher interest on certain accounts provided you leave the balance in the account for a specified length of time. Another variation allows you to direct the bank to automatically transfer money from your savings account to your checking account (in the same bank) to cover any overdrafts in the checking account.

Savings banks are permitted to give higher interest rates than commercial banks. Keep this in mind and check out interest rates before giving your savings business to any bank.

Loans

Loans are available for making costly purchases of goods or services—such as buying or remodeling a home, buying an automobile, or financing an education—or to help out in times of severe financial need.

When, or if, you apply for a loan, the lender will ask you the reason for the loan. The purpose of the loan will affect the type of contract, the length of time allowed for repayment, the interest rate, and even whether the loan should be granted.

Sometimes, collateral is required by the lender. Collateral is anything of value that a bank accepts as security against the repayment of a loan. Stocks, bonds, savings account passbooks (with balances at least equal to the amount borrowed), and other marketable property are used as collateral. If you do not repay the loan, the lender is legally entitled to take the collateral as payment.

If someone cosigns your loan, they are legally responsible to pay if you should default.

Loans should be undertaken only when absolutely necessary.

CREDIT

We live in a credit-oriented society. People who don't have enough readily available cash use consumer credit to help pay for home furnishings, cars, home appliances, clothing, vacations, remodeling, medical bills, and even old debts.

Why Use Credit Cards?

Convenience   Credit cards, in effect, are a ready means to obtain an unsecured loan. That is, by establishing your credit you're able to buy things without paying cash and without putting up property in exchange for the loan. With some credit cards you can get a cash advance as well. You maintain a good credit rating by establishing reliability through timely payments.

Instant Credit   As a reliable credit card holder, one who pays regularly and spends within the limits established by a credit card company, you can buy things without delay.

Emergency Use   Because you do have instant credit, you're able to charge things that you need or want unexpectedly. If you run low on cash while vacationing, a credit card can bring relief. If you discover a bargain that you didn't anticipate, you can buy it.

Flexibility   The purchasing scope of credit cards has mushroomed in recent years. The bulk of credit card activity relates to retail goods, gasoline, restaurant meals and beverages, hotel and motel accommodations, and transportation. Yet there are instances of credit cards being used to purchase goods in supermarkets, to pay rent, cab fares, insurance premiums—even some political contributions have been charged!

Cash Substitute   A principal advantage of a credit card is that you don't have to carry around large amounts of cash. On many occasions you will also avoid the uncomfortable need to produce all sorts of identification when you want to pay by personal check.

Ease of Payment Credit card invoices are sent out once a month. You can pay for all purchases on any card with just one check or money order. This could save on banking charges and it's easier than making a lot of different payments. Credit card purchases also provide you with a permanent record of expenditures.

To use consumer credit efficiently:

1. Understand all the types and sources.
2. Use credit only for purposes that are consistent with your income, spending plan, and long-range goals.
3. Shop for the best plan and services and the lowest terms available to meet your needs.
4. Limit your use of credit to what can be repaid comfortably.
5. Fulfill your repayment responsibilities promptly.

Three Types of Credit Cards

Bank Card These are all-purpose cards with which you can pay for retail goods, meals, lodgings, transportation, and more, at over a million businesses throughout the United States and the world. Usually you can get a cash advance of $100 or more from participating banks.

Bank cards set limits on how much credit you can have. Typically, it's $500 (some accounts go much higher). You won't be allowed to charge beyond your limit. Stores are required to make a phone call to their bank card center for approval of any transaction above a certain amount.

A local bank may have its imprint on your card, but there are just two major bank card companies in the country, Visa and Master Charge.

Travel and Entertainment Card These include American Express, Diners' Club, and Carte Blanche. They're honored at many restaurants, hotels and motels, retail stores, airlines, and car rentals. Some travel cards also provide a toll-free phone service to guarantee hotel and motel reservations.

Although these companies don't impose official limits on the amount of outstanding debt you can have, they keep close tabs on your payment records. If you seem to be on a spending spree or are slow in paying, you may be asked to stop using the card until your account is clear. If matters get totally out of hand, you cannot use the card altogether, a serious blow to your overall credit rating.

One-Company Cards Here we have some variety. Most major gasoline and oil companies issue cards you can use only at their service stations; occasionally one company's card is also good at the stations owned by another company. Sometimes, these cards can also be used for hotels and restaurants. Many local department stores and national chain stores have their own cards. Some of these establishments accept bank or travel cards as well. There are also airline and auto rental company cards.

Is Credit Easy to Get?

It all depends upon overall credit worthiness. How is that determined? What happens when you apply for a credit account or a loan?

First, identification is required; for example, a driver's license, social security card, voter's registration card, employment identification card. Second, other personal information is necessary: place of residence, period of time lived there, whether you rent or own, place of employment, type of work, length of time employed, salary, where you bank, whether you have savings and checking accounts elsewhere.

This information is requested in an interview or on an application or both, depending upon the type of credit. This credit profile will help the creditor determine whether the prospective credit user can and will pay for the credit and/or merchandise that's in question.

To obtain credit, a future user must have a regular income, a good record of paying bills on time, and some financial resources (savings, automobile, life insurance, home).

A consumer's credit ratings begins the first time credit is used. It is strengthened when bills are paid promptly and regularly and when credit is used in amounts that can be safely repaid.

How to Get a Credit Card

You'll find bank card application forms at participating banks, stores, and other outlets. Travel card applications are available in restaurants and stores. One-company card applications can be found at retail stores and service station outlets.

All applications go through a credit check. Bank and gasoline cards are usually given to anyone with good credit standing, even though his or her income is relatively modest. The travel, car rental, and airline companies have stricter income standards—typically, at least $10,000 a year. Individual stores and chains set their own criteria.

What Do Credit Cards Cost?

The travel card companies charge an annual fee of from $10 to $50, but no interest on the amount charged on the card. You don't pay a fee for a bank card, but there is interest charged if

> *Note:* Sometimes charge account bills don't arrive until long after the billing date, giving you little chance to get your payment in before interest is charged. If this happens, don't just write it off to red tape. Complain immediately to the company or store. If these late mailings continue, it may not be red tape at all but an unethical scheme to get interest money that you shouldn't pay. If you feel that this is happening to you, contact your local office of the Federal Trade Commission (or State banking authority, for bank cards). Legislation is now pending to protect you from these unfair practices. But until its passage, you must rely on self-protection.

you haven't paid within a certain time—usually 25 days. The same is true of most retail store cards.

Liability in Case of Loss

If your credit card is lost or stolen and someone else uses it, your liability stops at $50. That's the law. As a matter of fact, if you notify your credit card company in time, you won't even be liable for the $50.

In any event, you should take the following precautions:

1. Keep a list of all cards and their account numbers, and the names, addresses, and phone numbers of the companies. Keep the list in a place separate from your cards. It's a good idea to keep two lists, one at home and one at your place of work. If your cards are lost or stolen, contact each company immediately by phone or wire. Then follow with a letter.
2. Carry your cards separate from your wallet.
3. Keep only those cards that you intend to use. Cancel, then cut in half, those cards that you seldom if ever use or the ones that duplicate others.
4. If you have many credit cards, it might be a good idea to consider credit card insurance.

The Department of Consumer Affairs for the City of New York has what it calls "some hard facts on 'easy' credit." They're practical thoughts on the subject of credit.

CREDIT CARD DO'S AND DON'T'S

Do

- shop for credit as carefully as you do for merchandise. Compare! The price of credit varies as much as the price of goods.
- find out the different sources of available credit. Compare the costs of borrowing from banks, credit unions, finance companies with the costs of installment buying.
- consider the possibility of trying to get a loan for the entire purchase.
- study the price tag on merchandise you're planning to buy in installments. It must tell you the interest rate in percentage (%) and the finance charge in dollars ($).
- make as large a down payment as possible if you do buy on the installment plan. Make your payments as large as you can to pay back as fast as you can.
- look for the Notice to the Buyer before you sign a contract:
  1) Do not sign this agreement before you read it, or if it contains any blank spaces.
  2) You are entitled to a complete copy of this agreement.
- read the contract carefully.
- demand a copy of the signed contract. Take it with you, and keep it in a safe place.
- know what the penalties are if you can't make your payments.
- protect yourself against unlawful harrassment by creditors. They are not allowed to threaten action which they have no legal right to take.
- inform the bank or finance company acting as collection agents if you have a justified dispute with a home improvement contractor and want to suspend your payments.
- know that if a lawsuit is brought against you for default of payments, it must be brought in the county *you* live in, or in the county where the purchase was made.
- be sure that you get your charge account statement in the mail 15 days before any finance charges take effect, so that you have time to pay your bill in full, if this is your practice.

(list continued on next page)

MONEY 127

CREDIT CARD DO'S AND DON'T'S

Don't

- believe there is any "easy credit." Only getting it may be easy—paying it back is always hard.
- buy on installment credit until you have looked into all the other possibilities.
- forget that for cash you can buy at a discount house.
- forget that the law demands that you have all the necessary information so that you know the total price you'll end up paying.
- be misled into thinking that many small payments will be easier. They will cost you more in the long run.
- be rushed into signing anything. If the bargain won't be there tomorrow, maybe you shouldn't grab it today.
- sign if there are any blank spaces that could be filled in later.
- misplace your contract. Without it, you'll have a tough time if any problems arise.
- despair! In an emergency you may be able to work out an arrangement with the seller or holder of the contract.
- be intimidated. Creditors are not permitted to garnishee your wages, or contact your boss *unless* there is a court judgment against you.
- let them tell you that they are not responsible for the contractor they financed. A new law says they are.
- believe that the seller can arbitrarily pick a distant court, just to make it hard for you to appear.

Checking Up On Your Credit

Over 100,000,000 credit files now exist in this country and, increasingly, people are discovering that their files contain inaccurate or out-of-date information that should be corrected or removed.

Thanks to the Fair Credit Reporting Act, you can now check into your credit file to determine whether any information should be changed to improve your credit standing.

Know Your Rights According to the Fair Credit Reporting Act, the FTC maintains (FTC Buyers Guide No. 7) that you have the following absolute rights:

1. To be told the name and address of the consumer-reporting agency that was responsible for preparing any consumer report that was used to deny you credit, insurance, employment, or to increase the cost of credit or insurance.
2. To be told by a consumer-reporting agency the nature, substance, and sources (except investigative type sources) of the information (except medical) collected about you.
3. To take anyone of your choice with you when you visit the consumer-reporting agency to check on your file.
4. To obtain all information to which you are entitled, free of charge, when you have been denied credit, insurance, or employment within 30 days of your interview. Otherwise, the reporting agency is permitted to charge a reasonable fee for giving you the information.
5. To be told who has received a consumer report on you within the preceding six months, or within the preceding two years if the report was furnished for employment purposes.
6. To have incomplete or incorrect information re-investigated and, if the information is found to be inaccurate or cannot be verified, to have such information removed from your file.
7. To have the agency notify those you name (at no cost to you) who have previously received the incorrect or incomplete information that this information has been deleted from your file.
8. To have placed in your file, and included in future consumer reports, your version of any unresolvable dispute between you and the reporting agency about information in your file.
9. To request the reporting agency to send your version of the dispute to certain businesses for a reasonable fee.

10. To have a consumer report withheld from anyone who under the law does not have a legitimate business need for the information.
11. To sue a reporting agency for damages if it willfully or negligently violates the law and, if you are successful, to collect attorney's fees and court costs.
12. Not to have adverse information reported after seven years. One major exception is bankruptcy, which may be reported for 14 years.
13. To be notified by a business that it is seeking information about you which would constitute an "Investigative Consumer Report."
14. To request from the business that ordered an investigative report more information about the nature and scope of the investigation.
15. To discover the nature and substance (but not the source) of the information that was collected for an "Investigative Consumer Report."

On the other hand, the Fair Credit Reporting Act does not:

1. Give you the right to request a report on yourself from the consumer-reporting agency.
2. Give you the right, when you visit the agency, to receive a copy of or to physically handle your file.
3. Compel anyone to do business with an individual consumer.
4. Apply when you request commercial (as distinguished from consumer) credit or business insurance.
5. Authorize any federal agency to intervene on behalf of an individual consumer.

How to Locate Your Local Credit Bureau (Agency) Once you have established credit, whether it be good or bad, you can be nearly certain that there's a credit profile bearing your name at your local Credit Bureau or Agency. The identity of that particular bureau is a carefully guarded secret of the credit bureau trade association: Associated Credit Bureaus, Houston, Texas. However, you can locate your local Credit Bureau on your own as follows:

1. Look in the yellow pages of your telephone book under CREDIT BUREAUS or CREDIT REPORTING AGENCIES. Now look for the following prefix: "THE CREDIT BUREAU OF" (name of the city you're in). Also be alert for the following key names: "CREDIT REPORTS, INC." and "CREDIT INFORMATION, INC." You may inquire by telephone whether your credit file is there.
2. Ask any local bank officer where your credit file may be located. If this information still eludes you, call your local Better Business Bureau or nearest Federal Trade Commission office.

If you decide to visit a Credit Bureau to check on your file, here is a helpful checklist.

CHECKLIST FOR VISITING A CREDIT BUREAU

Did you:

_____ Learn the nature and substance of all the information in your file?

_____ Find out the names of each of the businesses (or other sources) that supplied information on you to the reporting agency?

_____ Learn the names of everyone who received reports on you within the past six months (or the last two years if the reports were for employment purposes)?

_____ Request the agency to reinvestigate and correct or delete information that was found to be inaccurate, incomplete, or obsolete?

(checklist continued on next page)

MONEY 131

CHECKLIST FOR VISITING A CREDIT BUREAU

Did you:

_____ Follow up to determine the results of the reinvestigation?

_____ Ask the agency, at no cost to you, to notify those you name who received reports within the past six months (two years if for employment purposes) that certain information was deleted?

_____ Follow up to make sure that those named by you did in fact receive notices from the consumer bureau or reporting agency?

_____ Demand that your version of the facts be placed in your file if the reinvestigation did not settle the dispute?

_____ Request the agency (if you are willing to pay a reasonable fee) to send your statement of the dispute to those you name who received reports containing the disputed information within the past six months (two years if received for employment purposes)?

INSURANCE

Life

A person might buy life insurance for a number of reasons. The main one is to provide financial protection for those who rely on that person for some or all of their support. Then, too, cash values or guaranteed funds can be useful in middle or old age, as you will see.

In business, principals of corporations or partnerships often have life insurance policies naming each other as beneficiaries. This arrangement provides a surviving principal or principals with sufficient funds to buy the other partner's interest from the heirs.

For those who may have to accumulate a debt to obtain education, there are policies to help make certain that the indebtedness will be paid.

Whatever the reasons, you should be familiar with the different types of life insurance policies available today.

Straight Life Policy This type offers protection for an entire lifetime. The premium remains the same each year. In addition, this policy builds a cash value that you can redeem when you reach a specified age.

Limited Payment Life Policy This one protects for life but the premiums are concentrated into a specified number of years—usually 10, 20, or 30 years. Or, you may pay premiums until a certain age, usually 60 or 65 years. The premium is higher than for a straight life policy for the same amount of coverage because the period of payments is shorter. However, the cash value grows faster.

Endowment Policies These enable you to accumulate a sum of money, which becomes available to *you* at a certain date. Meanwhile, there is insurance protection for the full amount to those who depend on you, should you die before the end of the policy period. Endowments build the largest cash values of any type of life insurance policy.

Term Insurance Policies They provide life insurance coverage for a given period of time, which can be 5, 10, 15, or 20 years or to age 65. Some term insurance policies are renewable at the end of the term, but the premium will be higher each time it is renewed. Most term insurance policies do not accumulate cash values.

Some policies combine the features of two types of insurance to meet special needs. There are *family income plans* that combine life and term insurance to provide greater family protection at low cost while children are young.

Retirement Income Policy This policy combines life insurance with provision for a lifetime income. It guarantees income for a beneficiary before that income begins.

Annuities

Annuities are sold by life insurance companies but they are not life insurance. Whereas the primary purpose of life insurance is to protect dependents, an annuity is designed to provide the owner with a guaranteed retirement income for life.

There are two kinds of annuities: *straight life* and *refund*. With the straight life annuity, payments stop when the owner dies. Refund annuity payments are made to a beneficiary if the owner dies before receiving the amount paid into the annuity. Straight life annuities cost less than comparable refund annuities but pay a large income since they are on the life of one person only.

Tax-shelter annuities are a relatively recent development for people employed in certain charitable, educational, and religious organizations. Up to a given level, a portion of one's salary allocated to these annuities is not taxable as current income. The effect is to lower income taxes during the earning years.

Another new development is the *variable annuity*. As with the regular annuity, it provides a monthly income for life. However, the funds behind the variable annuity are invested in common stocks. Thus, retirement benefits may vary from month to month although they will not fall below a given amount. Most variable annuities are available on a group basis through employers, but some life insurance companies are now making these available to individuals.

To some, perhaps many, people, insurance terminology is awesome, even incomprehensible. To avoid "small print-itis," a phobia that may stay with you forever if you're not careful, you should select an insurance company and agent that inspire confidence and make you feel comfortable. Ask for explanations of everything you don't understand. Don't agree to any policy until you fully understand it and are completely satisfied with its provisions.

Health

Accidents and illness are two unpredictable possibilities in your future. You don't like to think about them but you should.

Most people prepare themselves by having health insurance coverage. If you've ever had to pay a medical bill without the aid of health insurance you know how wise it is to be covered.

There are six kinds:

1. *Hospital expense insurance* helps pay for hospital room and board, routine nursing care, minor medical supplies, and related services.
2. *Surgical expense insurance* helps pay for the cost of operations.
3. *Physician's expense insurance* helps pay for in-hospital visits by a doctor and, depending on the policy, for home and office visits.
4. *Major medical expense insurance* helps pay bills for serious or prolonged illness or injury in and out of hospital.
5. *Dental expense insurance* helps pay for normal dental care and, depending on the policy, dentures, orthodontics, and annual checkups.
6. *Disability income insurance* helps to replace earnings you lose when you are unable to work because of illness or injury.

Hospital, surgical, and physicians' expense insurance provide basic coverage. Major medical and disability income coverage provide more extensive benefits.

If you work full-time, you probably have some basic protection under a group plan through an insurance company, Blue Cross, Blue Shield, or some other type of insuring organization. Many group plans also include major medical insurance. Maximum benefits of such protection usually range from $20,000 to $100,000 or more and help pay for almost every type of care and treatment prescribed by a physician, both in the hospital and at home.

Most major medical insurance policies have a "deductible" feature, which means that you pay bills up to a certain amount before the insurance company takes over. The deductible amount can range from $50 to $1,000. The higher the deductible amount, the lower the cost of the insurance.

Dental expense insurance is growing more popular. It is usually available on a group basis.

Disability insurance provides continuing income that will help pay the bills that never seem to stop—rent, food, electricity—when your salary stops.

Auto insurance, which you may be anticipating at this point, is covered in Chapter 7.

INVESTMENTS

Once you have planned for basic protection needs, regular living requirements, and money for emergencies, you may want to invest in stocks, bonds, and other securities to earn additional capital, interest, or dividends.

No single investment offers the utopian combination of maximum safety, steady income, high return, and potential growth. Generally speaking, the higher the return, or the higher the growth potential, the greater the risk to your money.

Securities

The three most common types of securities for individual investment are common stocks, preferred stocks, and bonds.

Common and Preferred Stocks

Common stock is the Number One security, basic to all corporate business and to our whole free enterprise system. When you buy a company's common stock, you become a stockholder in that company. In effect you're a part owner. What part you own depends on how many shares you own in relationship to the total number of shares that exist.

You invest in a certain company because you think it makes a good product and it is likely to make money. If *it* does, then *you* stand to make money. This can happen through the payment of dividends and/or through the increase in the market value of the stock.

Common stock is considered riskier than preferred stock but it does offer more favorable growth potential. In other words, common stock is subject to greater fluctuation than preferred stock.

As the name implies, *preferred stock* assures preferential treatment for its owner. It assures that the owner has a prior claim on all assets after all debts have been taken care of, should it ever be necessary to liquidate the company. It also accords a priority in the payment of dividends. On the other hand, as we said, the price usually doesn't fluctuate as much as common stock. So, while a preferred stock-holder might not enjoy dramatic increases, he or she is not as vulnerable to sharp decreases. Thus, it provides a more steady income security than do common stocks.

Bonds

Essentially, a bond is an I.O.U. Bonds are issued by corporations, the U.S. Government, and municipalities. A bond is held by the lender as proof that he has loaned a specified amount of money. You invest in bonds not for growth potential but for steady income in the form of interest payments. Therein is the difference between stocks and bonds. A stockholder, as a part owner in a company, expects to collect dividends and can further profit when the market value of his stock goes up. The person who buys a company's bonds is a creditor, not a part owner, and expects to receive a *fixed* return on his investment (although interest rates on some bonds can fluctuate). So you can see that bonds are a more conservative, less risky investment than stocks.

Should you buy bonds or maintain a savings account? It's a good question that should be asked of a banker or stock broker. Some bonds have often paid higher interest than savings, but it's not always that simple. So, investigate it thoroughly. For one thing there are different types of bonds, such as corporate, long term issues or treasury bonds, treasury bills with maturities as short as 91 days, certificates ranging up to a year, notes that may run up to seven years, and savings bonds (Series E and H) that are never traded in any market and never suffer any fluctuation in interest payment.

The Trading of Stock

A stock exchange is simply a marketplace where people buy and sell stocks every day through authorized agents or brokers.

The price of a stock is established when buyers compete with other buyers for the lowest price. It's more or less like an auction where bidder and seller conclude a transaction at a price that is mutually the best that both could get at that moment.

What Does It Cost to Buy Stocks?

Generally, the commission charged on stock transactions averages out to be about 1%. However, it could be as high as 6% if the order is for less than $100 worth of securities. If you have a large order, you should do some comparison-shopping for commission costs. Some brokers charge less than others.

Finding and Dealing with a Broker

If you don't know the name of a broker, one of your friends or associates might. Otherwise, look in the financial section of your daily newspaper. Decide which firm seems to have the policy you like and the service you need. Then visit your choice. Just drop in; you don't need any formal introduction.

Some consumers are awed by the brokerage business. Actually, it's not high-hat at all. So don't be shy, and don't be defensive if your potential investment is only several hundred dollars. Small investors are being encouraged more than ever.

When you introduce yourself and your finances to a broker, be candid. The more you tell the broker about your finances—your income, your expenses, your savings, your insurance, your obligations such as mortgage or tuition payments—the better he or she will be able to plan an investment program that is suited to you as an individual.

Listed and Over-the-Counter Stocks

To be listed on a registered stock exchange, a company must meet certain qualifications. There are many companies that cannot meet these requirements but they are sanctioned by the Securities and Exchange Commission (SEC) to issue stock and they become part of the over-the-counter market. Companies that do meet the requirements may choose not to be listed with a stock exchange, and may elect the over-the-counter method of selling, as well. In other words, over-the-counter stocks are not traded on the floor of an exchange but rather through a massive network of telephone and teletype wires that link together thousands of securities firms in the United States and abroad.

The chief attraction of the over-the-counter market is that you might find a future Xerox or IBM. There's an air of speculation about over-the-counter investments. Yet there are securities of some very solid companies—for instance, banks, life insurance, and fire and casualty insurance companies—

being traded every day on an over-the-counter basis. So don't form stereotypes until you've checked out the securities that are recommended to you by a broker or that are of particular interest to you.

TAXES

Preparing Your Tax Return

On the first day of January every year the countdown for tax returns begins. Invariably, thousands of people wait until the last minute. Some even apply for special extensions. It's not a wise habit, because you may overlook something important in the rush.

Forms

1040A, commonly referred to as the short form, is recommended by the Internal Revenue Service for taxpayers who have earned less than $10,000 and have no unusual tax deductions. With it comes an automatic 15% deduction for the filing taxpayer.

If your income is about $10,000 and you have some sizeable deductions—bad debts, heavy medical expenses, real estate sales losses, large contributions, certain business expenses that you paid with personal funds, for example—then by all means file a long form or *1040*. There are also lots of Supplemental Treasury forms like Form 2106 (Statement of Employee Business Expenses) and Form 2120 (Multiple Support Declaration). But let's just stick with 1040.

Before putting pencil to paper, gather all documents that will have bearing on your return. Start with your W-2 form (or forms, if you had more than one employer during the taxable year). You should have two copies of each. Copy B is the one you send in with your return.

Check the list of permissible deductions that comes with form 1040 and make sure you're not overlooking anything.

Read all instructions carefully, then have a dry run. In other words, make out one return in pencil, look it over, double check your figures, use it as a worksheet. When you're completely satisfied with your worksheet, transcribe your figures onto a final form, the one that you will actually send to the Internal Revenue Service.

Who Must File?

Each year, the tax laws change slightly, with increases or decreases in deductions or in definitions of non-taxable situations. Check with your local Internal Revenue Office (it's listed in the phone book) to find out whether you—in your particular situation—must file. In general, however, if you're independent, supporting yourself with a job, and have no extraordinary deductions, you probably have to file an income tax return.

COMMONLY ASKED QUESTIONS ABOUT TAXES

Q. What is F.I.C.A. tax?
A. It's Social Security tax. The maximum amount to be paid each year by an employer may change from year to year. In any one year, it's possible that an individual who has worked for more than one employer might have paid more than the maximum. Add up F.I.C.A. deductions from all W-2 forms. If the total exceeds the maximum for the year, claim a refund or credit.
Q. If you've had your tax return for the previous year prepared by a professional, can you deduct the expense this year?
A. Yes. If you itemize your deductions.
Q. Will the IRS still figure your tax on request?
A. Yes, if your adjusted gross income is $20,000 *or less* and it came only from wages, salary and tips, dividends, interest,

(questions continued on next page)

MONEY

COMMONLY ASKED QUESTIONS ABOUT TAXES

pensions, and annuities; if you claim the standard deduction; and if you file by the due date. The IRS will compute your taxes, regardless of the amount of your income, if you file by the due date on short form 1040A, and your income came only from wages, salary and tips, dividends, and interest.

Q. Is it true that a student can be exempt from income tax withholding?

A. Yes. Students and other individuals are exempt from tax withholding if they did not owe tax last year, expect to owe none in the current year, and have filed a Withholding Exemption Certificate (Form W-4E) with their employers.

Q. Is it possible to reduce the amount of tax withheld from your pay?

A. Yes. In addition to claiming all exemptions to which you are entitled, you may qualify for the special withholding allowance. Incidentally, if you are afraid that you will owe money at the end of the taxable year and can't bear to face that possibility, you can always have *more* tax withheld from your pay by claiming zero dependents. Some people who have had difficulties managing their money have tried this successfully. You get less money from week to week. But at the end of the year you may very well wind up with a refund rather than owing the government money.

Q. Are scholarships taxable?

A. If you receive a scholarship or fellowship grant, you may exclude all or part of that amount from your gross income, depending upon whether or not you are a degree candidate. However, a scholarship that is compensation for past or future services or primarily for the grantor's benefit is not excluded from gross income.

Q. When should you report interest earned on Series E Savings Bonds?

A. Only when the bonds mature or you cash them—whichever is earlier.

Q. What tests must be met for a taxpayer to claim a person as a dependent?

(questions continued on next page)

COMMONLY ASKED QUESTIONS ABOUT TAXES

A. All five of the following tests must be fulfilled:
   1. You must furnish over half of the dependent's total support during the calendar year.
   2. If the person's gross income is more than the current amount allowed for a dependent's earnings, you may not claim him or her as a dependent unless he or she is less than 19 years old at the end of the year or a full-time student during some part of each of five months of the year.
   3. The person must be a member of your household and live with you for the entire year or he or she must be closely related to you.
   4. In most cases, he or she must be a U.S. citizen or resident.
   5. The person must not file a joint return, unless one is not due but was filed merely to obtain a refund.

Q. Must every taxpayer who is eligible for the short form (1040A) use it?
A. No. It's always optional.

Q. If you have to pay for transportation to a doctor's office or a hospital, is this deductible?
A. Yes. You may deduct bus, train, air, and taxi fares as well as ambulance costs. You may deduct gas, oil, tolls, parking fees.

Q. Must you use the tables in the IRS tax forms package to compute a sales tax deduction?
A. Using the table is optional. If you don't, be sure to keep records of actual sales tax.

Q. Can you deduct bank credit card and oil credit card finance charges?
A. Yes. They're deductible as interest and so are charges levied by retail stores on customers' revolving charge accounts and designated finance charges.

Q. Are there any upper limits on how much you can deduct as a charitable contribution?
A. In general, contributions to most charities, such as churches, educational organizations, and hospitals, may be deducted in an amount up to 50% of your adjusted gross income. Contributions, like all deductions, should be supported by evidence (e.g. cancelled checks) of the donation, in case of an audit.

MONEY

TAX RETURN TIPS

1. Before you file have someone else check your return for arithmetic goofs. You could avoid a 6% annual interest charge—and possible penalties. Another idea is to take your return to an office where you have access to an adding machine or calculator and double check your addition by machine.
2. If you can't pay all the tax owed when it's due, file anyway and work out payments with the IRS. You may pay some penalty but you're not in criminal violation. And don't fall into the trap of not filing one year because you failed to file the previous year. If you have done this already, then make a voluntary disclosure of tax evasion. It's the unofficial policy of the IRS to allow the person to make amends without fear of prosecution. Before a tax disclosure, you should contact a good tax attorney.
3. If you are to meet with IRS representatives over a tax question or discrepancy, don't get unnecessarily uptight about the meeting. If you are pleasant and candid, you'll receive courteous, fair treatment.
4. If you are audited, don't panic. An audit doesn't automatically mean you'll owe more taxes. The IRS is just asking you to prove that you filed your return correctly. Occasionally people who have been audited have actually discovered that they're entitled to a refund.

LEGALITIES

Finding a Good Lawyer

Somewhere along the way, sooner or later in your life, you will need the services of a lawyer. When you buy a house, you have to close the deal and that requires the expertise and services of a lawyer. You may find yourself in a position where you will have to make a claim for damages against another party, or someone may make a claim against you.

Getting the right lawyer is not simply a matter of picking a person or firm that has all the right credentials and knows all the legal tricks. Legal matters are usually very personal. To represent you properly a lawyer must know a lot about you in relation to the action at hand. Very often this opens up rather intimate segments of your life, so you must feel comfortable with your lawyer. If your lawyer expresses understanding and sympathy or interest in your particular case, the chemistry is probably right. If you are handled impersonally or treated as though you and your case are not very important, that's a warning signal to switch attorneys.

When you're searching for a lawyer it's good to tap as many sources as you can for a recommendation. Very often the source will be an indication of the type of lawyer who's being recommended.

The ideal lawyer should offer a mixture of specialties: good negotiator, litigator, tax expert, and maybe even marital counselor. So, with this in mind, ask friends you respect and admire, your doctor, even a respected religious leader.

If, after the first consultation with a lawyer, you believe you've made a mistake, do the wisest thing: pay the consultation fee (it could range from $0 to $100) and find a replacement. In the long run it's worth the expense to be rid of an attorney who does not meet your standards. Find out ahead of time if the lawyer charges a fee for the first consultation.

How to Sue in the People's Court

Most people have heard of the Small Claims Court (almost all states have one). But the majority don't investigate its advantages, or else they think it's not for them. It's for the people and provides a simple, fast, and practically free way to reclaim at least part of your losses.

To start proceedings it's best to go to the office of the Small Claims Clerk (for the address, look in the telephone book under state or city courts or call your local Bar Association). You'll be told whether your case falls within the jurisdiction of the Small Claims Court. If it does, you must limit your claim to the maximum set by each state. If you're not 21, you must take along a parent or legal guardian.

You then file a claim that names the person you are suing and the reason for the suit. A small filing fee is charged.

The clerk will set a trial date and notify the defendant. The hearing will be held before a judge or a lawyer acting as arbitrator; there is usually no jury. Remember to bring any proof or witnesses to support your case.

Legal Aid Society

If you cannot afford a lawyer but need representation, each state has a Legal Aid Society that will appoint a lawyer to represent you if you meet the requirements. The requirements change from time to time, so check with your Legal Aid Society to find out whether you are eligible. In general, however, you cannot own property, stocks, or bonds, and there are firm—and low—limits on how much money you earn and how much you have in the bank.

Power of Attorney

A situation may arise during which you have urgent personal affairs to attend but, because of sickness, absence, or other reason, you are unable to handle things yourself. You may need to ask someone else to take care of these affairs for you. If legal or financial matters are involved, it might be necessary for this person to have power of attorney to act for you.

Full power may be granted, or the authority may be limited to certain functions such as making bank deposits and withdrawals from a checking account.

In any event, power of attorney is a very serious matter and must be given a great deal of thought. A lawyer will be able to advise you if there is any real need for you to take this step.

Keeping Important Documents and Papers

As you become more involved with life, you will no doubt accumulate papers and documents that have significance and value. If they are not judiciously filed in a central location, they have a way of disappearing. Once they do, they will be difficult to replace. On page 148 is a chart that will help you set up a system for handling such papers.

In this age of photocopies, it's a good idea and very easy to keep a copy of your important documents at home while the originals that deserve greater security are snugly stored in a safe deposit box at the bank. The reverse holds true, too. If you must have your original document at home, stash a photocopy at the bank.

Wills

To many people, especially those who are having the time of their lives, the subject of a will is morbid. Nevertheless, it is an important document if you are to manage all phases of your life.

There is nothing tricky about drawing up a will. Anyone who meets his or her state requirements (in most states you have to be 21 years old; in some, 18) can do it. It doesn't even require a lawyer although legal assistance is definitely recommended. The law recognizes any piece of paper that you have clearly labeled *will* and signed in the presence of two witnesses (who should not be beneficiaries) as long as you have complied with the mandatory requirements of your state. This is where the expertise and experience of a lawyer becomes a near necessity.

The legal charge for a simple will varies, but it is not very expensive.

A will is advisable even if you have only a few possessions (assets). It gives you the undisputed power to leave things to people of your own choosing. If you don't have a will, your property automatically goes to your parent(s) or next of kin. If

SAFETY OF IMPORTANT DOCUMENTS

Document	Keep in Safe Deposit Box	Keep at Home
Birth and death certificates	X	
Marriage license	X	
Adoption papers	X	
Divorce agreements	X	
Citizenship papers	X	
Military service records	X	
Passport		X
Diplomas		X
Social security card		X
Deeds and title papers to property	X	
Records of mortgage payments, repairs and improvements, purchase price, closing costs, and selling costs	X	
Savings certificates and passbooks	X	
Titles, bills of sale, payment records for auto	X	
Records of stocks		X
Records of bonds		X
Records of pension or profit sharing plans		X
Records of savings accounts		X
Insurance policies and records	X	
Income tax returns (also records of deductible expenses with receipts, records of income, records of payments)		X
List of credit cards and numbers		X
Canceled checks		X
List of checking accounts and account numbers		X

you don't want it this way, a will allows you to specify a beneficiary—and an executor—other than a parent or next of kin.

When you have a will, it should be periodically reviewed with your lawyer. You may have a change of heart. Also, wills should be changed to keep up with revised tax laws.

5 LEISURE

At-Home Entertaining

People to Meet

Places to Go

AT-HOME ENTERTAINING

The key to good entertaining is planning and organization. A good host or hostess is both a producer and a director.

Your first consideration is your guest list. The best food and drink can't save a gathering that has poor social chemistry. If you are bringing together people who have enjoyed each other's company in the past, your guest list requires no further analysis. On the other hand, if some of your guests are new to one another, indulge in a little constructive psychology.

Consider whether the interests and backgrounds of your guests make for a good mixture. A party can be disastrous if people can't or won't communicate.

If your guests are meeting for the first time, you can't predict exactly how they'll mix. But you can build in some safeguards.

Don't overload your party with one interest group that might automatically band together in conversation, excluding other guests. People meeting for the first time probe for a common interest or activity. When they find one, they explore it. Thus, if twelve of sixteen people come from the same business or background, they will use this common interest to communicate. Soon the four remaining guests become outsiders.

Make sure you circulate and keep conversations going. Since you will know more people in the room than anyone else, you know the topics of interest to your guests. If someone is hanging back, have them pass a tray or assist you in some other way that will bring them into contact with others.

Create a good atmosphere. People create auras; they give off "vibes." Other people sense them and a mood is established. When you're giving a party, your aura is the one that counts the most. It's not that you're more important than your guests. The fact is that it's your place and your party, and guests who accept these conditions put themselves in your hands for a certain amount of time.

It is your responsibility to be as cordial, charming, and relaxed as possible. This should come naturally since you are probably giving the party to be with your friends.

Of course, there are times when you may be tense from daily, unexpected pressures or from a sudden disagreement with a friend, relative, or roommate on the day of your party. Only if it is quite serious or too unshakable should you cancel your party at the last minute. Otherwise, put the problem aside temporarily and go on as planned. Very often, the charm that you had to manufacture at first will begin to flow naturally after awhile. Tensions may very well disappear for good as you begin to enjoy your own party. You owe it to yourself and your guests to give them the best of you, not the worst.

Some people tend to become edgy before a party. It's understandable, especially if you haven't entertained too often. Is everything going to be perfect? Well, if you've planned properly, chances are that things will go very well. Perfection? Well, you should strive for it, but don't come apart if some details fail to follow your pre-party plans. Just relax. Don't compensate for your jitters by not being yourself. Putting on airs is very different from creating an aura.

So, as host or hostess, always remember and apply one of the most vital truths of independent life—you're never better than when you're yourself. Don't get hung up on stereotypes. Successful hosts or hostesses don't have to be gourmet cooks or sparkling conversationalists. What is indispensable in the make-up of a good host or hostess is the ability to be considerate about guests (before and during the party) and responsive to them within the context of the social environment that he or she has created. The criterion is to enjoy your guests and have your guests enjoy you and appreciate your efforts.

Once you've decided whom to invite, you must decide whether to send invitations or make telephone calls. To get the highest percentage of acceptances, give your guests ample notice. Invitations should be sent out or telephoned ten days in advance. Seven days is cutting it close. Less than a week is rude—it implies that people have nothing else to do. The ten day advance period is ideal because it gives your guests enough time to make their own arrangements. Single guests who are invited with a date have sufficient time to ask the right person. Married couples with children can arrange for baby-sitters. Others who have tentative travel plans might want to manipulate their schedule to attend your party. If they can't, you have enough time to find replacement guests.

Last-minute party plans make it hectic for everyone and are often self-defeating. Better not to have a party at all than to ad lib one into chaos.

When you invite your guests, they may ask how they should dress. If attire is not understood by the very nature of the party, then you should be specific. Most parties now are casual. People seem to relax more when they dress in leisure clothes. However, if you have other ideas, make certain that every guest is aware of them. It would be uncomfortable for one guest to be dressed in evening clothes while all others are wearing denim or corduroy.

Giving a Dinner Party

A dinner party is a sit-down-at-the-table affair, so you should first decide how many guests you can seat comfortably at your table. Then decide whether you can actually cook for that many people. Once that's decided, invite your guests, and be sure to tell them that it's a dinner party. Most importantly, tell them what time they should arrive.

Then you can settle down to planning the party. The party that's planned perfectly is the one that functions without the guests becoming conscious of all the planning. The different phases of a party should flow into each other. The host or hostess should never appear to be strained. Most importantly, the one who is in charge of cooking or preparing the food should never get lost in the kitchen. This can be accomplished by planning a menu that requires that only a minimum amount of work be done after the guests arrive. In the table on page 154 are some rules for this kind of planning.

GUIDELINES FOR PLANNING A DINNER PARTY MENU

1. Plan every detail of your menu in advance. Consult friends, relatives, and cookbooks for ideas. Write down the menu and make your shopping list. Simple, well-cooked meals with which the cook is familiar are preferable to experimental recipes. If you want to whip up something new, whether it be an appetizer, entree, or dessert, prepare it for yourself at least once before the party. If it turns out well and you're confident that you can repeat it without a hitch, then you can include it in your menu with the assurance that it won't cause a crisis.
2. Avoid repetition of foods within the same meal. If fish is to be the appetizer, don't use it as the main course.
3. Make sure your meal contains a variety of textures, colors, and tastes. Balance firm and soft foods, select items with complementary colors, and include something sweet and something tart, something hot and something cold.
4. Plan menus that do not complicate either the use of the oven or refrigerator storage. All foods to be cooked in the oven should require the same oven temperature. There should be ample space in the refrigerator to accommodate all cold dishes.
5. Do as much as possible in advance. Dishes that can be cooked ahead of time and be either frozen or refrigerated until needed are a great convenience. On the day of the party, the table can be set and raw vegetables and salad fixings can be prepared hours in advance.
6. Make a timetable to determine your cooking order. Start with the dish that takes the longest, then the next longest, and so on. This kind of timetable will allow you to serve each element properly cooked and at the proper time. Be sure serving utensils and platters are ready to use.

Set the table as neatly and attractively as possible. Avoid crowding. The tablecloth should be spread so that the middle crease is up and it divides the table exactly in half with the edges hanging evenly all around the table. Placemats may be used instead of a tablecloth. It's a matter of personal taste.

If you have a centerpiece on your table, make sure that it

doesn't obstruct anyone's view. Candles placed at each side of the centerpiece can add a touch of formality or intimacy.

Plan your timing so that you will be ready to serve the food about half an hour after the time you asked the guests to arrive. This lets the guests get acquainted before you seat them at the table, allows any late-comers to arrive, and gives you a chance to do last-minute things in the kitchen.

Seat the host and hostess at opposite ends of the table. The person who's most responsible for serving the meal should be seated at the end nearest the kitchen. This will save steps.

Arrange your guests around the table, keeping their interests and tastes in mind. Try to place together those who will be congenial. Usually, you alternate men and women. Some people prefer to separate wives and husbands. That's up to you and your guests. The best seating arrangement is the one that's the most enjoyable for everyone.

If You're Serving Wine

In recent years, wine has become one of America's favorite alcoholic beverages. Wines should be chosen to complement the menu. There are three basic kinds: natural, sparkling, and fortified.

Natural wine is made by fermenting the juice of freshly squeezed grapes. As the name indicates, this is a totally natural process and it produces either a red, white, or pink wine that is mild in flavor and moderate in alcoholic strength (about 9 to 14 percent alcohol by volume). Natural wine is often referred to as table wine since it is generally consumed with food.

Sparkling wine is made by bottling the wine before the fermentation is quite finished, so that some of the natural carbon dioxide is trapped in the bottle. This technique creates bubbles. The best-known sparkling wine is Champagne.

Fortified wines are made by adding brandy to make a sweeter wine. The addition of the brandy increases the alcohol content to 15 to 21 percent by volume. Sherry and Port are two of the better-known fortified wines.

SELECTING A WINE

Wine Classification	Basic Types	Wine and Food Combinations
Aperitifs	Sherry (dry) Vermouth	Serve before meals chilled. Good with hors d'oeuvres.
White	Chablis (Burgundy) Sauterne Bordeaux White Rhine wine	Serve well-chilled with chicken, fish, shellfish, egg dishes, even veal.
Red	Red Burgundy (Beaujolais) Bordeaux Red Chianti Rosé	Serve at cool room temperature with steaks, chops, roasts, game, cheese dishes, pasta. Rosé can be served with white or red meats.
Dessert	Angelica Muscatel Cream (sweet) Sherry Port	Serve with dessert, chilled or at room temperature. Good with fruits, pastries, cake or cheese.
Sparkling	Champagne Asti Spumante Sparkling Burgundy Cold Duck	Serve well-chilled. Great with any course: appetizer, entree, dessert. Fine for any occasion, even no occasion at all.

The above chart will help you select the right wine to go with the food you're serving.

There is a rule of thumb, as indicated in the "Selecting Wines" chart, that matches up white wine with white meat; red wine with red meat; and rosé (pink) with either meat. Don't hesitate to break the rule. Each individual should decide which wine gives him or her the most enjoyment with certain foods.

It is customary to serve aged red wines at room temperature (65°F–75°F), dry wines and rose cooled, and sweet wines and Champagne cooler still. The theory goes that when wine is icy the flavor is deadened. Again, it's up to the individual. Many people prefer white wines and rosés served thoroughly chilled.

Wine is appreciated most when served with food, so make sure it's easily available by placing the bottle or carafe on the dining table and allowing guests to serve themselves. If you are serving more than one wine at the meal, the dryer wine should precede the sweeter one, and the lighter wine should come before the heavier one.

To help you understand more about wines, here is a glossary of wine.

GLOSSARY OF WINE

Aperitif: Literally means appetizer. Refers to a wine that is served before meals (sherry, Madeira, vermouth).
Beaujolais: Very popular French red table wine from Burgundy.
Bouquet: The fragrance that originates from the fermentation and aging of wine.
Brandy: A spirit produced from the wine of fresh grapes.
Brut: Extra dry.
Chablis: A dry, delicate white wine made in Burgundy, France.
Champagne: Sparkling wine. Name comes from region near Rheims, east of Paris.
Chianti: A ruby-red, dry Italian table wine made in Tuscany.
Claret: A designation for almost any red table wine.
Dry: A wine which is not sweet; also any wine having 14% or less of alcohol.
Fruity: Having the fragrance and flavor of the grape.
Madeira: A class of fortified wines from Madeira, a Portuguese island.
Mellow: Soft with some sweetness.
Port: Originally a sweet, heavily fortified wine from northern Portugal. Now there are many American Ports.
Rhine Wine: A term that originally referred to any wine from the Rhine Valley in Germany. In the United States, any white wine with less than 14% alcohol may be labeled Rhine.
Rosé: Means "pink" in French. It's a young wine that doesn't require much aging.
Sauterne: Golden white, full-bodies, fragrant wine.
Sherry: Gold- or amber-colored wine originally from Jerez near Seville, Spain. One of the finest aperitif wines. Also excellent for cooking.
Tart: Possessing agreeable acidity.

Additional Ways to Entertain Guests

A dinner party is not the only way to entertain at home. Buffets, brunches, cocktail parties, theme parties, and informal "Bring Your Own" evenings are some of the alternatives.

Buffet A serve-yourself *buffet* is an informal way to entertain guests when space is limited. Just make sure that each guest has a comfortable place to sit and a sturdy surface for his or her plate and glass. No one should have to balance a sagging or slippery plate and a handful of silverware for the sake of informality. Set up card tables or provide sturdy lap trays. Eating while sitting on the floor is okay if you have a low table; if you don't, guests will probably place their glasses on the floor and inevitably a glass will be knocked over or broken.

The buffet itself should be set out on a large, sturdy table that is covered by an appropriate cloth. A long narrow table placed against one wall works well, although a round, square, or oblong table will do, too.

Arrange the food and utensils so that the traffic will move in one direction. For example, have plates and silverware available at one end of the table, and the main dish and accompaniments next in the order in which you wish your guests to serve themselves. It is customary to avoid food that requires the use of a knife, although poultry, ham, and other meats are often served. Dessert and coffee can be placed on a separate table or sideboard.

Keep in mind that, although a buffet is versatile for serving larger groups, you should not invite more guests than your home can accommodate comfortably. Parties that are too crowded are more a sign of your lack of consideration than of your popularity.

Brunch *Weekend brunches* are becoming more popular because they offer great informality and a distinctive kind of relaxation. A brunch is more of a celebration than a breakfast. You can serve elements of both breakfast and lunch at the meal, which means the menu has great flexibility. Also, brunch doesn't have the time restrictions of a weekday lunch which must often be terminated because of business appointments. Since the weekend brunch is strictly a leisure-time activity, you have the latitude of serving beverages other than the traditional coffee, tea, milk, and juices.

In planning brunches, there are all sorts of food possibilities at your disposal—anything from scrambled eggs to blintzes, from eggs benedict to french toast. For best results, offer items from brunches that have pleased you in the past or consult one of the many cookbooks on the subject.

Cocktail Party *Cocktail parties* are usually short-term parties at which beverages and hors d'oeuvres are served. If such a party is preceding a dinner, a great variety and quantity of food is not only not necessary, but if you overload your guests with hors d'oeuvres, dinner will be anticlimactic. If no dinner will be served, you should plan on six to ten hors d'oeuvres for each guest, depending on the length of the party.

Don't try to supply hot hors d'oeuvres unless they can be served piping hot. Tiny, attractive canapes and dips for vegetables are much safer. If you're on a very tight budget, even bowls of nuts and potato chips or a simple dip and crackers will suffice.

When it comes to drinks, consider your guests. If you know the preferences of certain guests, you should do your best to have those ingredients on hand. Be sure you're supplied with one or more non-alcoholic beverages, such as fruit juices, soft drinks, tea, or coffee. Without these alternatives available, you are, in effect, punishing non-drinkers.

Theme Party *Theme parties* are built around one major idea or theme. They may involve decorating your apartment in some unusual way, serving the cuisine of a particular region or country, having guests come in costume, and so on. A pizza party is one of the easiest theme parties to host. All it takes are some good friends, beverages, and a call or visit to your local pizzeria. If you're especially ambitious, you could even attempt making your own.

LEISURE

Bring Your Own *"Bring Your Own"* parties are often the most fun. They are especially informal and suited to guests who are good friends. When there is coordination of what each guest is responsible for bringing, the food can be as exquisite as any sit-down dinner and a lot less expensive for the host or hostess.

The sample menus opposite may give you ideas for the different types of entertaining you might try at home.

When The Party's Over

After your guests have left, roll up your sleeves and head for the kitchen. Resist the temptation to leave the mess for the morning. It will take much longer to clean up if you let food dry on the plates and utensils.

Scrape waste from the dishes, rinse them, and empty and rinse the cups. Group everything according to type—all plates together, all glasses together, and so on. The largest plates should be on the bottom of the dish pile. Cups should be by themselves. Silver articles should be together, as should steel forks, knives, and spoons.

Use cold water to soak dishes that have been used for milk, eggs, fish, and starchy foods. Use hot water for dishes that have been used for sugar substances and for sticky, gummy substances like gelatin. Greasy dishes of all kinds, including knives, are more easily cleaned if you wipe them first with soft absorbent paper.

Wash dishes in the following order: glassware, silver, cups and saucers, plates, platters, serving dishes, cooking utensils. Slip glasses and china sideways into a pan or sink that is half-filled with hot water containing soap or detergent. Hot water should touch the outside and the inside of glassware and china at the same time to avoid the danger of cracking.

If dishes are very greasy, add a little washing soda or ammonia. Rinse all dishes in clean, hot water. Drain them, and wipe them dry with clean, dry towels if necessary.

BUFFET DINNER
Fruit Punch
Baked Chicken
Rice with Sautéed Almonds
Garden Salad
Raspberry Sherbet
Assorted Cookies
Beverages

BRUNCH
Sliced Melon
Scrambled Eggs with Sausage
Broiled Tomato Slices
Bran Muffins
Beverages

COCKTAIL PARTY
Beverages
Fresh Vegetables with Yogurt Dip
Assorted Cheeses with Crackers
Swedish Meatballs
Pineapple Wedges
Mixed Nuts

THEME PARTY
Spanish Fiesta
Guacamole Dip with Corn Chips
Chili
Shredded Lettuce
Tortillas
Flan
Beverages

PEOPLE TO MEET, PLACES TO GO

One of the most vital and on-going explorations in independent life is the act of meeting people who can offer meaningful friendship, intellectual stimulation, pleasurable romance, and engaging companionship. When you meet a person who fulfills all of these needs, check your heart and pulse rate. You're probably in love. Beyond this kind of very special, deeply intimate one-on-one relationship, each person needs to develop friendships with other people who share common interests. The question often asked is: "Who are these people and where do I find them?"

First of all, know yourself—know what pleases and displeases you. Armed with this knowledge, you should evaluate people you meet according to whether they meet your standards. Trying to conform to other people's standards is an inexcusable self-insult. No one is more important to you than yourself.

Friends Of Friends

If you already have a group of friends, the best way to meet additional acquaintances is through them. Although it's not foolproof, the theory here is that you are apt to get along with people who are liked by the people you like. However, when someone decides to play cupid on your behalf, you may experience some boring or unpleasant afternoons or evenings.

If you find yourself in a situation like this and it's an obvious disaster, bear with it. Put yourself in the other single's place. He or she may be going through the same agony.

Parties that offer mobility are much better. You arrive uncommitted and you can leave the same way. On the other hand, you may meet someone who interests you. If you don't, but still enjoy the sociability, then the party ends up a success.

Where You Work

You accept a job because of what it will do for your future. Of secondary importance is the question of what it will do for your current social life. However, in the case of a tie (two opportunities with equal potential), choose the employer whose personnel composition attracts you more. It can be disheartening for a single person to be completely surrounded by older and/or married people eight hours a day, five days a week. Some singles who are turned off by this environment eventually become disinterested in their jobs. When that happens, nothing is gained. But don't discount older and married people entirely. They have friends and interests, too, and can be invaluable friends to a single person. In fact, it's nice to have friends with different ages and lifestyles.

Traveling

There are two kinds of travel to consider: business and pleasure. Both can produce new acquaintances, but neither should be looked upon solely as friend-finding missions. You'll meet more people socially, either through business or on vacation, when you're not pushing it. People with a sense of desperation are usually ignored or exploited.

When you plan to travel to a location that doesn't offer the promise of easy sociability, ask friends if they have friends there. This may lead to something as interesting as having coffee with a stranger, or as memorable as an unexpected romance.

Your own out-of-town business contacts may be a good "meeting" source. They might be happy to introduce you to some of their friends.

When you plan a vacation (there will be more about that later), ask friends, check with travel agents, and keep your ear to the ground. There are many exciting places to visit. Often, meeting people comes naturally within the context of a vacation (ski lodge, poolside, boats, and trains). Travel clubs put people together, too. Investigate them if this appeals to you. If you're interested in finding a date, don't give the impression you can't live without one. It's a sure turn-off.

Clubs

There are singles' clubs in existence that offer skiing, dancing, tennis, golf, cocktail parties, or tours. They often sound as though there couldn't be a more appropriate meeting ground. Married people and older singles cannot join, so you are assured of being among your peers. Check the singles' clubs in your locale. But be sure you get a look at their facilities, members, and activities before committing to a contractual fee. Some singles find these clubs to be too high powered, and the setting too contrived and dedicated to the hunt. Other singles love them. It's a matter of personal preference.

Politics

Politics is a field that's crying for dedicated young people. If this kind of involvement is at all appealing to you, expect a social bonus. During an election year there are all sorts of volunteers, many of them single. The excitement of the race becomes contagious. A common cause abounds and so does togetherness. You're sure to meet some people who will interest you.

Religious and Charitable Organizations

Many of these groups have clubs and programs tailored to the needs of singles. Many have both educational and social activities.

Sports

Participation sports are now the thing. Besides being highly beneficial to health, they're also excellent door-openers to new relationships. Ski slopes and tennis courts are good meeting places. So are beaches, lakes, ice skating rinks, jogging paths, bowling alleys, and parks. You also can meet people while sailing, horseback riding, playing golf, or spectating at race car rallys and other sports.

Adult Classes

Although you may have finished school and are now working, you may want to take some courses to fill the gaps in your education. Continuing education courses are offered by colleges, libraries, high school adult programs, and practicing professionals in various fields. You may be attending to learn something new and rewarding, but you may also develop new friendships with other students.

Your Building

If you live in an apartment building or a multiple dwelling, you're bound to see neighbors who interest you either visually or through bits of conversations overheard in hallways and elevators. Wait for the opportunity and open a conversation. It may begin with a neighborly hello or a mention of the weather (if that opener isn't dead yet). What it may lead to is an invitation to a party, brunch, or movie.

Singles' Bars

Here you have to be careful. Many singles' bars are like mass feedings and the soup de jour is superficiality. Take them for what they're worth. Enjoy them if that's your preference.

Many participants have admitted that there is little substance in single saloon society. But some have been lucky. They've enjoyed themselves and occasionally found people whom they've enjoyed meeting. Regulars are usually more interested in themselves than the people they meet. Don't feel alienated if you don't enjoy these encounters.

The essence of meeting people is to develop enjoyable relationships. These can make your life pleasurable. However, be alert to friendships that begin to deteriorate because of incompatibility, lack of respect, or growing inconsideration. Discuss the problem candidly with the other person. If the situation is irreversible, then dissolution of the relationship is better for both parties. Even if it's traumatic, it is better than long-term misery.

Through experimentation, openness, and a total awareness of yourself, you'll soon know the types of places and the kinds of people that are for you.

PLACES TO GO

When You're Planning to Travel

One of the joys of the independent life is the freedom to travel. Traveling provides the opportunity to see and experience unforgettable places and to meet new and exciting people.

A major decision in planning a trip is whether to travel alone or with a friend. In many ways it is similar to asking yourself whether you want to live alone or have roommates. In both cases, the answer is very personal. Ultimately, you must decide what's best for you. The object of traveling is self-enjoyment. Since you're doing it on your time and with your money, the pleasure should be yours, too. Compromises are fine, but if you agree to a disagreeable itinerary for someone else's sake, you'll start your trip on the wrong foot and probably end it that way, too.

SHOULD I TRAVEL ALONE OR WITH A FRIEND?

Traveling Alone
- You can do what pleases you exclusively.
- You can have a true solo experience.
- You can meet new people strictly on your own terms.
- You can make unilateral decisions; no compromises.
- You can be by yourself whenever you want to be.

Traveling With A Friend
- You probably won't be lonely.
- You can split costs and live more economically.
- You can share experiences.
- Often, interaction is a catalyst for finding new places and doing something that you normally wouldn't do on your own.
- Very often it's easier to go places in groups of two or more.
- If another person knows more about a certain place, language, or people, it can add to the travel experience.

The length of your trip and your destination may have some bearing on whether you go alone or with a companion or group. Quick weekends are less critical than longer vacations. Still, you should weigh your decision carefully, and consider the above factors.

If you decide to travel with a friend, both of you should take equal responsibility in planning the trip. This will prevent any possible bickering on the trip about selection of transportation, land accommodations, or destinations.

Evaluate your similar interests so that your compatibility is enhanced. Be candid about dissimilar interests and agree to split up occasionally if those interests draw you in different directions. Stay loose. Be considerate of one another. A good joint vacation should end with the participants wanting to travel together again.

Deciding Where To Go

There are so many exciting places in every part of the world that deciding where to go is difficult. Consider your interests, your available time, and the amount of money you're able to spend. Narrow your choices to two or three areas that seem appealing, and research them thoroughly.

The library is a good source of books on travel and on specific countries or areas. A travel agent can provide you with free travel brochures and some expert advice that should help you make a final decision. Foreign government tourist offices may also have some information. Included on pages 169–170 is a list of these offices and their addresses.

Arranging Your Trip

Once you decide where you want to go, you must go about getting there. A good idea is to consult an accredited travel agent. Travel agents are experts in figuring air routes, itineraries, reservations, and costs. They sell on a commission basis, earning their fee not from you but from the companies (air lines, hotels, car rental agencies) whose services they employ on your behalf. Since they represent a variety of carriers, hotels, motels, guest houses, and organizations, they can tailor a trip to your needs, wishes, and budget. They're also well versed on escorted and independent package tours, if that's to your liking. But to say that all travel agents are complete experts is to generalize. Not all travel agents know every nook and cranny of the world. An agent may recommend a hotel from a brochure, a listing, or even from hearsay.

Evaluate the agent as you're discussing your trip. Don't be afraid to ask the agent if he or she has been to your vacation spot. The answer may be revealing. If the agent is familiar with it, he or she will begin to fill in with details. The conversation will be telling, and if it tells you that this travel agent knows what he or she is talking about, then you can relax. You're in capable hands.

FOREIGN GOVERNMENT TOURIST OFFICES

Australian Tourist Commission
1270 Avenue of the Americas
Suite 2908
New York, N.Y. 10017

Austrian National Tourist Office
545 5th Avenue
New York, N.Y. 10017

Bahamas Tourist Office
30 Rockefeller Plaza
New York, N.Y. 10112

Bermuda Government Official
 Travel Information Office
630 5th Avenue
New York, N.Y. 10020

Canadian Government Office
 of Tourism
1251 Avenue of the Americas
Room 1030
New York, N.Y. 10020

Ceylon Tourist Board
609 5th Avenue
Room 308
New York, N.Y. 10017

Czechoslovak Travel Bureau—
 Cedok
10 East 40th Street
New York, N.Y. 10016

Dominican Tourist Information
 Center Inc.
485 Madison Avenue
New York, N.Y. 10022

Egyptian Government Tourist
 Office
630 5th Avenue
New York, N.Y. 10020

Finland National Tourist Office
75 Rockefeller Plaza
New York, N.Y. 10019

French Government Travel
 Office
610 5th Avenue
New York, N.Y. 10020

German National Tourist Office
630 5th Avenue
New York, N.Y. 10111

Greek National Tourist
 Organization
645 5th Avenue
New York, N.Y. 10022

Haiti Government Tourist
 Bureau
30 Rockefeller Plaza
New York, N.Y. 10020

India Government Tourist
 Office
15 North Mezzanine
30 Rockefeller Plaza
New York, N.Y. 10112

Indonesian Consulate General
 and Information Office
5 East 68th Street
New York, N.Y. 10021

Irish Tourist Board
590 5th Avenue
New York, N.Y. 10036

Israel Government Tourist
 Office
350 5th Avenue
New York, N.Y. 10118

Italian Government Travel
 Office
630 5th Avenue
Suite 1565
New York, N.Y. 10020

Jamaica Tourist Board
866 2nd Avenue
New York, N.Y. 10017

(list continued on next page)

LEISURE

Japan National Tourist
  Organization
45 Rockefeller Plaza
New York, N.Y. 10020

Kenya Tourist Office
60 East 56th Street
New York, N.Y. 10022

Lebanon Tourist and
  Information Office
405 Park Avenue
New York, N.Y. 10022

Malaysian Tourist Center
420 Lexington Avenue
Room 2148
New York, N.Y. 10170

Mexican Government Tourism
  Office
405 Park Avenue
New York, N.Y. 10022

Moroccan National Tourist
  Office
521 5th Avenue
New York, N.Y. 10017

New Zealand Consulate General
630 5th Avenue
Suite 530
New York, N.Y. 10111

Panama Government Tourist
  Bureau
630 5th Avenue
Suite 1414
New York, N.Y. 10011

Polish National Tourist Office
500 5th Avenue
Room 328
New York, N.Y. 10110

Puerto Rico Tourism Company
1290 Avenue of the Americas
Room 3704
New York, N.Y. 10104

Romanian National Tourist
  Office
573 3rd Avenue
New York, N.Y. 10016

Russian Travel Bureau Inc.
20 East 46th Street
New York, N.Y. 10017

Scandinavian National Tourist
  Office
75 Rockefeller Plaza
New York, N.Y. 10019

Spanish National Tourist
  Office
665 5th Avenue
New York, N.Y. 10022

Surinam Tourist Bureau
1 Rockefeller Plaza
Room 1408
New York, N.Y. 10020

Swiss National Tourist Office
608 5th Avenue
New York, N.Y. 10020

Turkish Government Tourism
  and Information Office
821 United Nations Plaza
New York, N.Y. 10017

Venezuelan Government Tourist
  Bureau
450 Park Avenue
New York, N.Y. 10022

Virgin Islands Government
  Tourist Office
10 Rockefeller Plaza
New York, N.Y. 10020

Yugoslav Travel Agency
Centroturist
509 Madison Avenue
Room 1604
New York, N.Y. 10022

Try not to carry a lot of cash when you travel. Invest in traveler's checks for most of your money. They usually cost a small amount, but it's well worth it, since they can be replaced if they're lost or stolen. When you purchase the checks at your bank, write the check numbers and amounts on the form you receive, and put the form in a safe place in your luggage, *not* with the checks. Mark off the checks you cash each day so your records are current. If you lose any checks, contact the issuing agency immediately and report the amounts and numbers of the lost checks. The company will issue new checks to replace the lost ones.

In fact, you may find that you don't need to carry much cash. For example, most restaurants, stores, trains and airlines, hotels, tourist atttractions, and so on in larger cities all over the world will accept traveler's checks instead of cash. You will need cash, however, for small expenditures such as tips, newspapers, local transportation, quick informal meals, purchases in some smaller stores, and in some of the less tourist-oriented small towns. The amount of cash you need to carry also varies from country to country. Check with your travel agent or ticket agent. Only you can decide—with experience—how much cash you need to carry, but remember that if you lose cash, it's gone forever.

You may also have your vacation planned for you by joining a private travel club. For a membership fee of $20 and up you can become a member. These clubs offer travel packages, often at very reduced rates. The more substantial clubs offer their members nominally priced activities such as cocktail parties, wine tasting parties, group lunches, backgammon instruction, tennis lessons, squash clinics, and more.

Be sure the travel club that attracts you is a legitimate one. If you have any doubts, contact your local Better Business Bureau.

Obtaining A Passport

A passport is an official document that is issued by your government and that identifies you as one of its citizens. If you are traveling overseas, you will need to show your passport in each country you enter. Some foreign countries also require a visa, or stamp of approval, to be affixed to your passport. Others waive this formality.

You may apply for a passport by appearing before a passport agent at one of the passport agencies in Boston, Chicago, Honolulu, Los Angeles, Miami, New Orleans, New York, Philadelphia, San Francisco, Seattle, or Washington, D.C. You may also apply with a clerk of any federal court or state court, or a judge or clerk of any probate court. You'll be asked for proof of citizenship, so bring a birth certificate, an expired passport, or a baptismal certificate. You'll also need to bring an official passport photo—one taken according to Custom's requirements and not more than six months old. A passport is valid for five years, after which it must be renewed.

If you lose a valid passport, you should report it immediately to the Passport Office, Department of State, Washington, D.C. 20524 or, if you're abroad, to the nearest consular office of the United States.

Health Precautions

Vaccinations are no longer required for travel to many areas. However, consult your physician for recommendations as to which shots are advisable for certain countries. If you visit a country and didn't get all the necessary shots first, you not only risk getting sick, you also will not be allowed back into the United States until you've waited out a quarantine period.

In some unindustrialized countries, drinking the local water or eating uncooked fruits and vegetables can cause severe diarrhea. When you travel in these areas, drink bottled water or the distilled water found in the better hotels.

Preparing To Leave

Experienced vacationers believe in traveling light, realizing that many items of apparel (socks, underwear) can be hand-

PREPARING A TRAVEL WARDROBE

1. Consider the climate at your destination. Use an almanac or encyclopedia for information on seasonal temperatures.
2. Determine whether your activities will be formal, informal, or both.
3. Choose easy-care clothes that are not bulky.
4. If your trip is more for sightseeing and touring than for socializing, leave expensive jewelry behind. Valuables are always a potential liability when traveling.
5. Work with one or two basic color schemes. This is the old mix-and-match logic. Sports coats and slacks, or skirts and blouses, can be interchanged to create a number of different looks. Bring along interesting accessories as well.
6. Keep your shoe wardrobe to a minimum. Shoes are bulky and often heavy. Make sure you have at least one very comfortable pair for walking.

washed along the way. Other items can be laundered by local cleaning services. Judging how many items and what weight clothing to take is a skill that is acquired with experience. However, above are some initial guidelines that will help you prepare your travel wardrobe.

Packing For The Trip

Try to limit the amount you are taking and, if possible, put everything into one suitcase. A cavalcade of luggage represents poor planning and means increased tipping of porters at terminals and hotels.

Choose lightweight luggage that has a comfortable grip. Bags with latches are preferable to those with zippers, which can break and make your luggage unusable. Some bags come equipped with wheels, or you can purchase a luggage caddy for under $10.00.

Working with a 26″ suitcase, a good size for traveling, pack the bottom layer with clothing that should be folded flat and smooth—slacks, shirts, blouses, dresses, and jackets. Alternate directions so the bulk is evenly distributed. Be sure to pack clothing on lightweight hangers. Place bulky items—shoes, toiletries, accessories—on top, and tuck small items like underwear, socks, and tee shirts in the spaces. It's a good idea, too, to pack clothes inside plastic cleaning bags to cut down on wrinkles.

When you reach your destination, unpack immediately. Since you've used hangers, suits and dresses can be hung in a closet without delay.

Another good idea is to save a plastic bag, knot it at one end, and use it as a hamper for your soiled clothes. If you must repack before cleaning these items, they will be separate from your clean apparel.

Useful Abbreviations and Conversions

When you begin to study guidebooks, brochures, articles, and hotel rate schedules, you may encounter the following abbreviations, which indicate the meal plans that are being offered:

EP: European Plan, meaning room only, no meals.
AP: American Plan, meaning room plus three meals a day. In Europe this is called full pension.
MAP: Modified American Plan, meaning room plus breakfast and either lunch or dinner. In Europe this is called demi-pension.
CP: Continental Plan, meaning room and breakfast. In Europe this means a light continental breakfast consisting of rolls and coffee; in the West Indies it means a full breakfast.
BP: Bermuda Plan, meaning room with a full course breakfast. In England, this is called B and B, which stands for Bed and Breakfast.

TRAVELER'S TIPS

1. Plan to arrive at the airport well ahead of time. Why begin a leisurely vacation by rushing frantically to catch a plane? Your airline ticket agent or travel agent will give you the check-in time.
2. Ask your airline agent or travel agent about transportation to air terminals. Taxis are great. But usually there are buses and limousine services, sometimes free but usually for a nominal fee.
3. If you plan to rent a car at your point of destination, arrange for it well in advance of departure.
4. Invest in traveler's checks, and keep the record of use up-to-date.
5. Many foreign-bound travelers find it convenient to exchange some of their money for foreign currency before leaving the United States. That's fine, but check on the total amount of foreign currencies that can be taken into a country. Your travel agent, ticket agent, and even larger banks can tell you.
6. We've already mentioned the potential problem of water in some foreign countries. It would be good preventive medicine to check with your doctor before leaving. He'll be able to prescribe some medication to take along for emergencies.
7. Take it easy until you're accustomed to the sudden changes in climate, altitude, and time.
8. Leave your itinerary with a close friend or relative in case of an emergency but stress that this precaution is strictly for *emergency* situations.
9. If you wear glasses, take along your lens prescription.
10. If you have a physical condition that may need emergency treatment, carry an I.D. tag, bracelet, or card.
11. Travel with an open mind. Leave behind any predetermined conceptions. Very often they turn out to be misconceptions.
12. Be sure that your home is in order before you leave—all lights off, all appliances unplugged, windows and doors secured, and newspaper and mail service stopped or picked up by a friend.
13. Begin to enjoy your vacation the minute you lock your front door.

METRIC EQUIVALENTS

Length

1 kilometer (km) = .6 mile

Temperature	*Customary Measure*	*Approximate Metric Equivalent*
freezing	32° F	0° C
mild weather	60° F	15° C
beach weather	80° F	26° C
body temperature	98.6° F	37° C

Since most European countries use the metric system of measurement, a few equivalents could help you. If, for instance, you order a liter of wine in France, you'll be getting a little more than an American quart. Above are some other helpful metric equivalents for use in your overseas travels.

Shopping for the correct sizes in shoes and clothing in Europe can be a problem, unless you have the information, in chart on page 177, on hand.

Customs Information

When you return to the United States from a trip abroad of at least 48 hours duration (no minimum time limit for Mexico), you are entitled to an exemption of duty (import tax) on $300 worth of merchandise providing you have not used the exemption or any part of it within the preceding 30 days. You may import articles in excess of the exemption, but you must pay duty on those items not entitled to free entry. If you are returning either directly or indirectly from the American Virgin Islands, American Samoa, or Guam, you have a larger exemption.

COMPARISON OF AMERICAN AND EUROPEAN CLOTHING SIZES

Men's Sizes		Women's Sizes—Dresses		
American	European	American	French	English
Shirts		10	38	32
13	33	12	40	34
13½	34	14	42	36
14	35-36	16	44	38
14½	37	18	46	40
15	38	20	48	42
15½	39	40	50	
16	40	42	52	
16½	41	44	54	
17	42	46	56	
17½	43			

American	European
Shoes	
6	38
6½	39
7-7½	40
8	41
8½	42
9-9½	43
10-10½	44
11-11½	45
12-12½	46
13	47

Women's Sizes—Shoes

American	English	European
4-4½	2-2½	34
5-5½	3-3½	35
6	4	36
6½	4½	37
7-7½	5-5½	38
8	6	38½
8½	6½	39
9	7	40
9½-10	7½-8	41
10½	8½	42
11-11½	9-9½	43
12	10	44

American	European
Socks	
9	23
9½	24½ (also Cadet)
10	25½ (also Page 2)
10½	26¾ (also Homme 3)
11	28 (also Demi Patron)
11½	29 (also Patron)
12	30½

You will not be able to bring home articles considered injurious to the general welfare. Obscene literature from abroad is banned, as well as lottery tickets, wild birds, endangered wildlife, liquor-filled candies, switch-blade knives, narcotics, fruits, plants, vegetables, livestock, meats, poultry, and pets from an area with high evidence of rabies. Diseased organisms and vectors for research or educational purposes require a permit.

For more details concerning customs regulations, write to the U.S. Customs Office, P.O. Box 7118, Washington, D.C. 20044.

Enjoying your leisure is only possible when you're in good health. The next chapter will give you tips for improving your physical condition and ensuring your well-being.

6 HEALTH

Getting In Shape

Finding a Doctor

Dental Care

Other Health Resources

GETTING IN SHAPE

Looking your best physically is another contributor to self-confidence when you are becoming independent. But, more importantly, being in shape helps you maintain your health.

Exercise is an important part of shaping-up. It needn't be boring, either. There are many enjoyable ways to firm up soft spots, become limber, improve your coordination, and build your endurance. Below are some of the activities you can choose from to improve your physical condition. They've each been given an exercise rating of excellent, very good, good, fair or poor.

Forms of exercise that require special facilities (i.e. tennis, racquetball, swimming) often cost money. Using public facilities, joining Y's, or registering in school adult fitness programs are some of the ways to keep expenses low.

Private clubs usually require membership and can be quite expensive. Don't join one of these until you're sure you've selected the right form of exercise for you. Many of these clubs register more members than their facilities can hold, knowing that some members pay their fees, then stop using the facilities after an initial spurt of interest.

Exercise cannot guarantee you a good shape if you're not eating properly. Overindulging or undereating are both potential problems.

Consult the chart on page 182 to find the ideal body weight for someone of your height and body structure.

Now that you know what your desired weight should be, you'll have to take steps to reach it if you're not already there. In addition to exercise, you'll probably need to change your eating habits in order to achieve the physical appearance you want.

Your body is constantly working to keep you healthy, and all that activity takes energy. Your body gets the energy from the food you eat. The amount of energy in any particular food is measured in units called Kilocalories—officially, one thousand times the amount of energy it takes to raise one cubic centimeter of water from 15° to 16° Centigrade. When food

FORMS OF EXERCISE

Archery: A sport for all ages and strengths. Little initial instruction required. Exercise rating: fair to good.

Bicycling: An invigorating outdoor activity for everyone. From the waist down, muscles get a workout. Good for lungs. Exercise rating: good to excellent.

Bowling: A relaxing indoor sport. Not much strain involved, especially for regular players. Good sport for camaraderie. Exercise rating: poor to fair.

Calisthenics: Programmed exercise. Dance may be considered a part of this. Exercise rating: excellent.

Golf: Outdoor sport that requires concentration, dedication, and eye-hand coordination. Not very strenuous, but a good test of determination. Exercise rating: fair.

Handball or Racquetball: Very strenuous sports. Require endurance, dexterity, and mobility. Exercise rating: good to excellent.

Ice Skating: A beautiful sport for indoors or out. Exercise rating: poor to excellent depending on skater's performance.

Jogging: Grueling, but beneficial to body and lungs. Should be done with regularity. Exercise rating: good to excellent.

Paddle Ball: Handball played with a paddle for more finesse and a greater range of shots. Exercise rating: good to excellent.

Sailing: A very satisfying form of outdoor recreation. Requires lessons; it's wise to know how to swim first. Exercise rating: good.

Skiing: A good escape from routine to outdoors. A social sport. Requires skill and coordination. It's a good idea to take lessons. Exercise rating: good to excellent.

Swimming: One of the most active and invigorating of all sports. Requires the use of many muscles. Exercise rating: excellent.

Tennis: Can be very energetic. Lessons recommended. Good exercise for entire body. Expands the lungs. Exercise rating: excellent.

DESIRABLE WEIGHTS FOR MEN AND WOMEN*

Weight in pounds according to frame (as ordinarily dressed, including shoes)

Height (with shoes on)		Men		
Feet	Inches	Small Frame	Medium Frame	Large Frame
5	2	116-125	124-133	131-142
5	3	119-128	127-136	133-144
5	4	122-132	130-140	137-149
5	5	126-136	134-144	141-153
5	6	129-139	137-147	145-157
5	7	133-143	141-151	149-162
5	8	136-147	145-160	153-166
5	9	140-151	149-160	157-170
5	10	144-155	153-164	161-175
5	11	148-164	157-168	165-180
6	0	152-164	161-173	169-185
6	1	157-169	166-178	174-190
6	2	163-175	171-184	179-196
6	3	168-180	176-189	184-202

		Women		
4	11	104-111	110-118	117-127
5	0	105-113	112-120	119-129
5	1	107-115	114-122	121-131
5	2	110-118	117-125	124-135
5	3	113-121	120-128	127-138
5	4	116-125	124-132	131-142
5	5	119-128	127-135	133-145
5	6	123-132	130-140	138-150
5	7	126-136	134-144	142-154
5	8	129-139	137-147	145-158
5	9	133-143	141-151	149-162
5	10	136-147	145-155	152-166
5	11	139-150	148-158	155-169

*"Overweight and Underweight," Metropolitan Life Insurance Company.

and diets are discussed, Kilocalories is usually shortened to KCal or just calories. If you supply more calories—more energy—than your body needs, your body uses what it wants and converts the excess to fat, storing it up for emergencies. If you supply too little energy—too few calories—your body makes up the difference by changing some of the stored fat back into usable energy. Each one-pound weight gain means that approximately 3,500 calories have been eaten in excess of the body's needs.

To lose a pound it is necessary to cut calories below the body's needs in order to use up the stored excess. It is best to plan on losing weight gradually. Many different reducing diets have been suggested as temporary ways to lose weight. None of these work over a long period of time unless your habits of eating are altered, at first to lose weight, and then to maintain your weight at the new level.

Special reducing diets (such as fasting or the high fat, low carbohydrate diets) should be undertaken only after consultation with a physician. However, it is possible for anyone to shed pounds by cutting down on the amount of food usually eaten. This will result in a regular, gradual weight loss. The amounts of proteins, vitamins, and minerals needed daily should be maintained while calories are reduced. This can be accomplished by following a balanced diet that includes lean meats, poultry, fish or eggs; fruits and vegetables; and skim milk or low-calorie cheeses.

In order to assess accurately whether you're eating less, you might want to keep track of the number of calories you're taking in.

The calorie values on the chart that follows are averages. They represent the most accurate generalizations possible, according to government and other authoritative nutrition sources. The calorie count of foods may be determined by calculating the calories of the basic components. These consist of proteins and carbohydrates, generally calculated at 4 calories per gram; and fats, calculated at 9 calories per gram. Calories of wines or liquors are computed on the basis of 7 calories per gram of alcoholic content (½ the proof equals the percentage of alcohol): there are 28.3 grams to an ounce.

CALORIE COUNTER

	Serving	*Calories*
ALCOHOLIC BEVERAGES		
Beer	12 oz.	144
Bourbon	1½ oz.	120
Brandy	1 oz.	75
Champagne	3½ oz.	90
Cider	6 oz.	71
Cordials:		
Anisette	1 cordial glass	74
Apricot brandy	"	64
Benedictine	"	69
Creme de Menthe	"	67
Curacao	"	54
Daiquiri cocktail	4 oz.	125
Gin	1½ oz.	107
Highball	8 oz.	150
Manhattan cocktail	4 oz.	167
Martini cocktail	4 oz.	145
Mint Julep	10 oz.	212
Old Fashioned cocktail	4 oz.	185
Planters' Punch	8 oz.	175
Rum	1½ oz.	105
Rye whiskey	1½ oz.	120
Scotch whiskey	1½ oz.	105
Tom Collins	10 oz.	180
Vermouth:		
French	3½ oz.	105
Italian	3½ oz.	167
BREADS		
Date Nut	1 slice	100
French	"	60
Italian	"	60
Pumpernickel	"	60
Raisin	"	60
Rye	"	55
White	"	60
Whole Wheat	"	55
Muffins:		
Blueberry	1 average	112
Bran	"	130
Corn	"	150
English	"	145
Whole Wheat	"	103

(calorie counter continues on next page)

CALORIE COUNTER

	Serving	*Calories*
BREADS		
Rolls:		
Hamburger	"	89
Hard	"	160
Parker House	"	115
Crackers:		
Graham	1–2½" in diameter	14
Salted	1–2" "	17
Soda	1–2½" "	25
Matzoh	1–6" "	78
Oyster	10 pieces	30
Ritz	1 piece	17
Rye Wafers	4 pieces	90
CANDIES, DESSERTS & SWEETS		
Apples baked, 2 tablespoons sugar	medium	200
Apple pie	⅙ of 9" pie	400
Applesauce with sugar	⅙ cup	115
Applesauce, unsweetened	⅙ cup	50
Blueberry pie	⅙ of 9" pie	370
Brown Betty	½ cup	172
Cake, angel food	3" slice	165
Cake, butter with frosting	2" slice	370
Cake, chocolate with frosting	2" slice	445
Cake, sponge	2" slice	120
Candied fruits:		
Apricots	1 average	101
Cherries	1 large, 2 small	17
Citron	1" square	89
Figs	1 piece	90
Ginger Root	1 piece	17
Grapefruit, lemon, orange peel	1 tbsp. grated	32
Pineapple	1 slice	120
Caramel candy	1 oz.	115
Cherry pie	⅙ of 9" pie	414
Chocolate eclair	1 average	320
Chocolate fudge	1" square	115
Chocolate pie	⅙ of 9" pie	300
Custard	½ cup	142

(calorie counter continues on next page)

CALORIE COUNTER

	Serving	*Calories*
CANDIES, DESSERTS & SWEETS		
Custard pie	⅙ of 9″ pie	325
Doughnut, baking powder	1 average	125
Doughnut, yeast	1 average	130
Flavored gelatin	½ cup	70
Gingerbread	2″ cube	175
Gumdrops	1 large, 8 small	33
Hard candy	2 sq., 2 rolls	38
Honey	1 tablespoon	65
Ice cream, chocolate	½ cup	180
Ice cream, vanilla	½ cup	145
Jam or Jelly	1 tablespoon	55
Jelly Beans	10 pieces	66
Lemon Meringue pie	⅙ of 9″ pie	356
Maple syrup	1 tablespoon	55
Marmalade	1 tablespoon	55
Marshmallow	1 oz.	90
Mince pie	⅙ of 9″ pie	340
Molasses	1 tablespoon	50
Pumpkin pie	⅙ of 9″ pie	260
Sherbet, orange	½ quart	152
Sugar:		
brown	1 tablespoon	45
confectioners	1 tablespoon	30
granulated	1 tablespoon	45
CEREALS		
Hot		
Farina	1 cup	140
Cream of Wheat	1 cup	130
Oatmeal	1 cup	148
Rice	1 cup	164
Wheat Germ	1 cup	245
Wild Rice	¼ cup	99
Ready to Serve		
Corn flakes	1 oz.	110
Bran cereal	½ cup	60
Raisin bran	½ cup	73
Puffed rice or wheat	1 cup	55
Shredded wheat	1 large biscuit	100

(calorie counter continues on next page)

CALORIE COUNTER

	Serving	Calories
DAIRY PRODUCTS		
Butter or margarine	1 pat	50
Butter or margarine	1 tablespoon	100
Buttermilk	1 cup	90
Cheese:		
Blue cheese	1 tablespoon	49
Blue mold	1 oz.	103
Brick	1 oz.	103
Camembert, domestic	1 oz.	84
Cheddar, American	1 oz. 1" cube	112
Cottage	½ cup	120
Cream	1 oz.	105
Edam	1 oz.	87
Gruyere	1 oz.	115
Parmesan	1 oz.	110
Roquefort	1 oz.	111
Swiss	1 oz.	105
Chocolate drink milk	1 cup	190
Cream:		
Coffee	2 tablespoons	60
Heavy	2 tablespoons	110
Half & Half	2 tablespoons	40
Sour	2 tablespoons	110
Egg, boiled	1 medium	80
Egg, fried with 1 tsp. fat	1 medium	113
Egg, scrambled	1 medium	110
Milk, skim	1 cup	90
Milk, whole fresh	1 cup	160
Yogurt, plain	1 cup	120
Blueberry	1 cup	220
Orange, strawberry	1 cup	151
Pineapple	1 cup	216
Prune	1 cup	254
Red Raspberry	1 cup	225
Spiced Apple	1 cup	245
Vanilla	1 cup	186
FISH & SEAFOOD		
Abalone, broiled	4 oz.	100
Clams, steamed	5 oz.	107

(calorie counter continues on next page)

CALORIE COUNTER

	Serving	*Calories*
FISH & SEAFOOD		
Cherrystone clams	6 clams	100
Codfish	4 oz.	180
Crabmeat, canned	3 oz.	85
Fillet of Sole	4 oz.	85
Fish sticks	5 sticks/4 oz.	100
Flounder, broiled	4 oz.	70
Haddock, broiled	4 oz.	135
Halibut, broiled	4 oz.	200
Herring	4 oz.	200
Lobster tails	4 oz.	100
Lobster, broiled	½ avg.	125
Lox, smoked	4 oz.	240
Mackerel, canned	4 oz.	205
Oyster cocktail	10 raw med.	80
Perch, broiled	4 oz.	130
Pike	4 oz.	90
Pompano, broiled	4 oz.	185
Red Snapper	4 oz.	100
Salmon, canned pink	4 oz.	160
Sardines, canned in oil	4 oz.	233
Scallops, broiled	1 svg.	140
Sea Bass	4 oz.	105
Shrimp, canned	4 oz.	125
Swordfish, broiled	4 oz.	200
Tuna, canned in oil	4 oz.	227
White Fish, baked	4 oz.	210
FRUITS & FRUIT JUICES		
Apple	medium	70
Apple juice	1 cup	120
Apricots, canned, sweetened	4 halves w/juice	105
Apricots, dried	4	39
Apricots, fresh	3 medium	55
Avocado	½ medium	185
Banana	1 medium	85
Blackberries	1 cup	85
Blueberries	1 cup	85
Boysenberries, canned	3½ oz.	38
Cantaloupe	½ of 5" melon	60

(calorie counter continues on next page)

CALORIE COUNTER

	Serving	*Calories*
FRUITS & FRUIT JUICES		
Cherries, canned	½ cup	115
Cherries, fresh	1 cup	40
Cranberry sauce	2 tablespoons	85
Dates	3 or 4	85
Figs, dried	1 large	60
Figs, fresh	3 small	90
Fruit cocktail, canned	½ cup	97
Grapefruit	½ medium	55
Grapefruit juice, canned	½ cup	95
Grape juice	1 cup	165
Grapes, green, seedless	1 cup	95
Guava	3½ oz.	62
Guava juice	4 oz.	86
Honeydew melon	¼ medium	35
Lemon	1 medium	20
Mangoes	½ medium	66
Nectarine	1 average	40
Orange	1 medium	75
Orange juice	1 cup	110
Peaches, canned	2 halves w/juice	90
Peaches, fresh	1 large	50
Pears, canned	2 halves w/juice	90
Pears, fresh	1 medium	100
Persimmons, Japanese, raw	3½ oz.	77
Persimmons, Native, raw	3½ oz.	127
Pineapple, canned	1 slice w/juice	90
Pineapple, fresh	1 cup, diced	75
Plum	1 medium	25
Prune juice	1 cup	200
Prunes, dried	1 large	17
Prunes, stewed	4 medium w/juice	75
Raisins, seedless	¼ cup	115
Raspberries, fresh	½ cup	35
Rhubarb, stewed	½ cup	192
Strawberries, fresh	1 cup	55
Strawberries, frozen	½ cup	124
Tangerine	1 average	40
Tomato	3½ oz.	22
Tomato juice	½ cup	24
Watermelon	1 slice (4" × 8")	115

(calorie counter continues on next page)

HEALTH

CALORIE COUNTER

	Serving	Calories
MEATS		
Bacon	1 6" strip	50
Beef, corned	3 oz.	185
Beef, corned, hash	3 oz.	155
Beef, filet mignon	4 oz.	400
Beef, hamburger	4 oz.	325
Beef, rib roast	3 oz.	375
Beef, sirloin	3 oz.	330
Beef, tongue	3 oz.	210
Bologna	1 slice	66
Frankfurters	1 average	155
Ham, baked	3 oz.	245
Ham, boiled	3 oz.	201
Lamb, roast leg	3 oz.	235
Lamb chop, broiled	4 oz.	400
Liver, beef	2 oz.	130
Liver, calf	1 slice (3" × 2¼" × ⅜")	74
Pork chop	3½ oz.	260
Pork roast	2 slices	310
Veal chop, loin	3 oz.	185
Veal roast	3 oz.	230
Veal cutlet	3½ oz.	277
POULTRY		
Chicken, fried	drumstick	90
Chicken, broiled	3 oz.	115
Chicken, fried	½ breast	155
Duck, roasted	1 slice (3½" × 2½" × ¼")	109
Squab, flesh only	3½ oz.	142
Turkey, roasted	2 slices (4½" × 2½" × ¼")	190
NUTS & NIBBLES		
Almonds	12–15 nuts	90
Brazil nuts	¼ cup	229
Cashew nuts	¼ cup	190
Chestnuts, fresh	2 large	29
Chestnuts, dried	1 cup	377
Chestnuts, shelled	½ cup	191
Coconut, dried	2 tablespoons	42
Filberts or Hazelnuts	10–12 nuts	97
Hickory nuts	15 small nuts	101

(calorie counter continues on next page)

CALORIE COUNTER

	Serving	Calories
NUTS & NIBBLES		
Macadamia nuts, roasted	6 whole	109
Peanuts	¼ cup halves	210
Pecans	¼ cup halves	185
Pistachio nuts	30 nuts	88
Walnuts	¼ cup halves	162
Cheese tidbits, crackers	15 crackers	81
Corn chips	1 serving	292
Popcorn, plain	1 cup	54
Potato chips	1 piece	13
Pretzels	3½ oz.	390
PASTA		
Macaroni, cooked firm	1 cup	207
Noodles, egg	1 cup	200
Pizza with cheese	3½ oz.	236
Spaghetti, cooked firm	1 cup	216
SOUPS		
Asparagus, cream of, canned	1 cup	110
Celery, cream of, canned	1 cup	122
Chicken noodle	1 cup	65
Clam chowder, Manhattan	1 cup	87
Mushroom, cream of	1 cup	120
Minestrone	⅓ can	72
Onion	⅓ can	37
Pea soup	1 cup	130
Tomato soup, cream of	1 cup	125
Vegetable (beef base)	1 cup	80
VEGETABLES		
Artichokes	1 medium	45
Asparagus	8 stalks	25
Beans, green	½ cup	15
Beets	½ cup	25
Broccoli	⅔ cup or 1 lg. stalk	26
Brussels sprouts	6 or ½ cup	22
Cabbage	½ cup, chopped	12
Cabbage, cooked	½ cup	15

(calorie counter continues on next page)

HEALTH

CALORIE COUNTER

	Serving	*Calories*
VEGETABLES		
Carrots	1 medium, raw	20
Carrots, cooked	½ cup	22
Cauliflower	1 cup	25
Celery	2 medium stalks	10
Coleslaw	1 cup	120
Corn, fresh	1 medium ear	70
Cucumber	½ medium	15
Green pepper	1 medium	15
Kale, cooked	1 cup	30
Lettuce	¼ large head	15
Lima beans	½ cup	90
Mushrooms, canned	½ cup	20
Mushrooms, fresh	10 small	15
Okra	10 pods	30
Onion	1 2½" diameter	40
Parsnips	1 cup	100
Peas, canned	½ cup	82
Peas, fresh cooked	½ cup	55
Potato, baked	1 average	90
Potato, boiled	1 average	90
Potato, sweet, baked	1 average	155
Potato, french fried	10 pieces	155
Radish	1 medium	1
Sauerkraut	1 cup	45
Spinach, cooked	½ cup	20
Squash, summer, cooked	½ cup	15
Squash, winter, cooked	½ cup	65
Turnip greens, cooked	1 cup	25
Watercress	1 bunch	10
Yams	½ cup	105
Zucchini, cooked	1 cup	30

FINDING A DOCTOR

Taking care of yourself requires more than getting in shape. Of all the facets of independent life, maintaining your health should be given primary consideration.

Medical views differ as to whether an annual check-up is necessary. But if you're moving to a new community, you should make the acquaintance of a local, family doctor who can hold your medical file. Although medicine is in an age of specialization, there are still family physicians (general practitioners) available. If an illness arises that requires treatment by a specialist, your family doctor will surely refer you to one.

To find a physician in a new community, consult your city or county medical society. Other sources include recommendations from friends, religious organizations, or a nearby hospital with a good reputation (teaching hospitals are preferred).

Some criteria to keep in mind when choosing a new doctor are:

1. Location—Can you reach the doctor fairly easily?
2. Confidence—Does the doctor seem knowledgeable? Can he or she communicate clearly? Do you feel comfortable in his or her presence?
3. Cost—Does the doctor's fee schedule seem reasonable?

Don't be intimidated when you meet with your doctor. Remember, you are paying the fees and are entitled to ask questions.

Women will need to find a local gynecologist as well as a family physician. Annual visits are recommended, especially if you notice anything strange, such as a lump on a breast or excessive vaginal discharge.

People of all ages should have their blood pressure checked regularly. High blood pressure (hypertension) is a dangerous condition, but it can be controlled with the proper medication.

DENTAL CARE

Dental checkups are important, too. Teeth are a part of your body, and can affect your health. Proper dental care also has cosmetic benefits. Don't allow yourself to be the kind of person who looks great until you open your mouth.

Six-month dental checkups are recommended. A good dentist who sees you on a semi-annual basis can keep cavity damage to a minimum and closely watch other problem areas you may have.

Although your teeth may be cavity-free and in good shape, they still require periodic cleaning to remove plaque, calculus, and tartar.

When you move into a new neighborhood, you can search for a dentist by contacting the local dental society. In large urban areas, dental schools are able to make recommendations. Other sources include your local hospital, your family physician, and your friends.

Be sure to have your dental records mailed to your new dentist. These records will provide your new practitioner with a blueprint of you. With your history in hand, your dentist will be able to deal with your problems more effectively.

HERE'S A HINT...

You can't save money by postponing appointments. It's amazing, but true, that many young people try to postpone regular dental checkups as a way of saving money. The sad truth is that people who haven't received thorough dental checkups for a few years are most likely to have serious and expensive dental problems.

If dental bills are ones you think you can't afford, you'd be smart to reconsider. Have a dental checkup every six months. It's much better to spend your money today to prevent major problems in the future.

OTHER HEALTH RESOURCES

Helping Professionals: Where to Find Them

In addition to doctors and dentists, problems arise that require locating other competent professionals. The following list contains some resources that may be of help to you:

Counselors

Community Council of Greater New York
225 Park Avenue South
New York, New York 10003

Family Service Association of America
44 East 23rd Street
New York, New York 10010

National Council of Family Relations
1219 University Avenue Southeast
Minneapolis, Minnesota

Young Men's Christian Association (YMCA)
291 Broadway
New York, New York 10007

Day Care Professionals

Daycare and Child Development Council
622 14th Street, N.W.
Washington, D.C. 20005

Dieticians

American Dietetic Association
430 North Michigan Avenue
Chicago, Illinois 60611

Environmental Experts

Office of Public Affairs
Environmental Protection Agency
401 M Street, S.W.
Washington, D.C. 20460

Family Planners

Planned Parenthood Federation of America
810 7th Avenue
New York, New York 10019

Home Economists

American Home Economics Association
2010 Massachusetts Avenue, N.W.
Washington, D.C. 20036

Insurance Experts

Insurance Information Institute
110 William Street
New York, New York 10038

American Council of Life Insurance
1850 K Street, N.W.
Washington, D.C. 20006

Psychiatrists

American Psychiatric Association
1700 18th Street, N.W.
Washington, D.C. 20009

Publc Health Professionals

American Public Health Association
Division of Program Services
1015 18th Street, N.W.
Washington, D.C. 20036

United States Public Health Service
5600 Fishers Lane
Rockville, Maryland 20852

(list continued on next page)

Information concerning product safety or personal health matters is available from the following:

Automobile Hazards

National Highway Traffic Safety Admin.
400 7th Street, S.W.
Washington, D.C. 20590

Breast Cancer

Breast Cancer Advisory Center
P.O. Box 422
Kensington, Maryland 20795

Child Abuse

Child Welfare League of America, Inc.
44 East 23rd Street
New York, New York 10010

Society for Prevention of Cruelty to Children
110 East 71st Street
New York, New York 10021

Flammable Fabrics

Flammable Fabrics Hotline
Consumer Product Safety Commission
800-638-2666

Gambling

Gamblers Anonymous
235 East 31st Street
New York, New York 10016

Product Safety

Product Safety Hotline
800-638-8326
800-492-8363 (in Maryland)

Rights (of the Disabled)

Disability Rights Center
1346 Connecticut Avenue, N.W.
Washington, D.C. 20036

Rights (of the Individual)

American Civil Liberties Union
22 East 40th Street
New York, New York 10016

Rights (of Patients in Hospitals)

American Hospital Association
840 North Lake Shore Drive
Chicago, Illinois 60611

Runaways

National Runaway Hotline
800-621-4000
800-972-6004 (in Illinois)

Venereal Disease

VD Hotline
800-523-1885
800-462-4966 (in Pennsylvania)

Consult your telephone directory for additional sources of assistance available to you locally. Some of these include:

Your Local:
Department of Consumer Affairs
State or County Medical Society
Food and Drug Administration Office
Social Security Office
Welfare Department
Legal Aid Society
Extension Service (U.S. Department of Agriculture)
Blue Cross/Blue Shield Office

7 EXTRA$

Owning a Pet

House Plants

Buying a Car

OWNING A PET

To own a pet seems so appealing. Cuddly puppies and fuzzy kittens look so wonderfully cute in pet shop windows. Friends and neighbors are constantly asking if you have room for a marvelous pet they are unable to keep. But, appealing as owning a pet may seem, it's no simple matter for a single person.

Pets can provide much joy and companionship, but there is an inherent responsibility that exists in an owner-pet relationship. Pet owners must feed, house, clean, and groom their pets on a regular basis. Not to do so amounts to neglect and cruelty.

Are you prepared to take on this responsibility? This is the question you must answer honestly before making a decision to take in a pet. If you have never owned one, seek advice. Ask friends who are owners. Talk to pet store people or breeders. Research the different kinds of pets and their corresponding needs. Investigate and compare their traits.

If you are convinced that you will be a responsible, loving pet owner, analyze your own personality and needs. Once you have done so, you should be able to determine what type of pet would be most compatible with your temperament and lifestyle. Don't fool yourself into thinking that a dog is a dog, or that all cats are alike. They have different personalities and instincts.

Selecting a Dog

Dogs can be friendly or shy, fawning or aloof, cheerful or grumpy, calm or nervous. Some foreign breeds that initially were in short supply but large demand have been grossly inbred, making many offspring high-strung and difficult to handle. Watch for signs of hyper-sensitivity and impatience. Select a dog as you would a friend—on the basis of its qualities.

Choosing between a male and female is a matter of preference. Some experts feel that a female tends to be more faithful and intelligent. But this shouldn't be a determinant. Consider, too, the cost of sex alteration if this is desirable.

From whom should you buy a dog? Very often a friend might offer one from a litter at a reasonable price or at no cost at all. There isn't an easier way to become a dog owner. But apply your rules of selection very objectively before saying "yes." Any puppy can win you over. Keep in mind that in no time at all that cute little creature will be an adult. If you disapprove of the full-grown species and decide to give the dog to someone else, the dog could be unfairly traumatized. Dogs are capable of giving love and loyalty. They're also quite capable of feeling rejection and in severe cases can go through a process that is akin to our mental breakdown.

Pet stores are a standard source for dogs. Check out the appearance of the shop and the attitude of the owner before buying. Be very careful. Some experts recommend buying from a kennel. Here, breeding is an art, and the chances of acquiring a very fine animal improve considerably.

Selecting a Cat

In general, dogs are more domesticated than cats, a difference that can make a cat more or less desirable, depending on your profile as a would-be pet owner.

Cats are quite independent. They are self-cleaning, their independent spirit allows them to be left alone with less owner concern, they don't have to be walked, and they can usually be left with friends without causing the cat much fear or trauma. Although their way of life puts less demands on the owner, they still require love and care.

When should you buy a cat? It takes a mother cat seven weeks to wean her kittens. If you wait until the kitten is that old, it's easier for you and better for the kitten.

Male or female? It's up to you. It tends to be easier to care for a female, since males have a habit of straying.

If you are interested in good blood lines and want a purebred cat, obtain your cat from a breeder, not a pet store. You can search out breeders by reading *Cats Magazine* or *Cat Fancy*. You can also contact breeders at local cat shows. If you're not that fussy about breeding, a pet store purchase or a purchase or gift from a friend can suffice.

Selecting a Bird

Birds are a complete departure from dogs and cats. You can curl up with a cat and pet a dog, but a relationship with a bird is different. Birds need affection like other pets, but they return it in their own way. Birds, once acquainted with you, may perch on your finger, arm, or shoulder. Others may talk to you or follow you from room to room

There are many species of birds available. Compare the qualities of each by reading books and visiting pet stores. When you've arrived at a final list, look closely at different birds of that species. If your choice is of a lively breed, then eliminate any birds that sit quietly amid festive activity. Chances are they're sick, and it takes skilled veterinarians to bring birds back to health.

Be sure to purchase a cage large enough that the bird can spread its wings. The spaces between the wires must be small enough to keep the bird inside. Check with your pet store owner or manager about food and toys. Parakeets love to look at themselves in a mirror and will spend considerable time talking to themselves in front of one.

Check about maintenance, too. Bird cages need to be cleaned regularly to prevent unhealthy odors. Some birds can be messier than others.

Selecting Fish

In terms of owner-pet relationships, fish are the most remote. Fish must be appreciated by the eye and the mind—the

BUYING AND MAINTAINING FISH

- Make sure the fish have no blemishes or injured fins.
- Consult your pet store owner or manager as to what selection would be most compatible.
- Don't overbuy. An overcrowded tank community makes for poor living conditions.
- Be sure to buy scavenger fish to keep the tank clean.
- Don't overfeed fish. One feeding a day is plenty. At each feeding give the fish only as much food as they can eat in five minutes. Turn on the aquarium light at feeding-time.
- Aquarium water should always be fresh.
- Decontaminate new plants before introducing them to the aquarium. Consider using plastic plants rather than live ones that foster the growth of algae.
- Don't put the aquarium too close to a window. Drafts can cool the water—fish chill easily and may die.
- Don't give your aquarium too much sunlight. It can raise water temperature and cause too much algae.
- Check the acidity (pH) and hardness of the water once each week. Pet stores sell kits for use in regulating these factors.
- Be sure that the sponges used to clean the aquarium and the buckets used to fill it are free of soap and other chemicals.
- Care for your aquarium according to the instructions that came with it.

experience can be fascinating and calming. A fish tank is a society and can be viewed as such.

Above are some tips for buying and maintaining fish.

Selecting Wildlife

In searching for unusual pets, some people consider and actually acquire wildlife species such as monkeys, small wildcats, raccoons, and snakes. Aside from the fact that it is illegal in many areas to keep wild animals as pets, experts strongly recommend against it, since wild animals raised from infancy have been known to suddenly turn on their owners. It is a foolish owner who pridefully feels that he or she has, with copious amounts of love, eliminated all the natural instincts of a wild creature. To avoid possible injury or heartbreak, be less creative and more pragmatic when selecting a pet.

HOUSE PLANTS

House plants have been increasingly popular over the past decade. When they are properly cared for, they are wonderful to look at and add beauty to any decor.

The best place to buy plants is a store that specializes in them. The so-called bargains that you find in supermarkets and cut-rate stores or from mail order firms are often poor specimens that have received rough treatment and lack of care. They often fail to survive and need to be replaced.

In shopping for a plant you must decide the type that appeals to you, the plant's requirements for survival, and the plant's overall condition.

Evaluate the amount of light in your apartment. Most window areas provide three types of natural light: 1) no direct sun, 2) a limited amount of direct sun—maybe an hour or so, and 3) full sun. Choose your plants accordingly (see the following chart for suggestions). The healthiest plant will wither quickly under improper conditions. If natural light is poor in your home, you might consider artificial light. There are special plant fixtures and bulbs available.

Before buying a plant, check it thoroughly for pests (look under the leaves and at the stem junctures). Pass up plants with unnaturally blotched, speckled, or yellow leaves. Foliage should have a healthy, green character.

LIGHT REQUIRED FOR SOME COMMON HOUSE PLANTS

No Direct Sun	*Limited Direct Sun*	*Full Sun*
Rubber Plant	Begonia	Geranium
Aspidistra	African Violet	Citrus
Sansevieria	Asparagus Fern	Sanseviera
(for foliage)		(for blossoms)
Maranta	Gloxinia	Verbena
Philodendron	Azalea	Euphorbia
Grape Ivy	Spider Plant	Grape Ivy
Fiddle-Leaf Fig	Rosary Vine	Coleus
Boston Fern	Grape Ivy	Rat-Tail Cactus
Bamboo Palm	Dieffenbachia	Aloe
Kentia Palm	Columnea	Aztec Lily
Pothos	Avocado	

CARING FOR HOUSEPLANTS

Watering

When you purchase your plant, ask your retailer how much water is needed and write this information on the bottom of the plant pot.

Periodically, poke your finger into the soil. If the soil is very dry, it's a sign the plant needs water. But don't overdo it. Overdoses can damage roots and ultimately cause deterioration of the entire plant.

Fertilizing

Most house plants need to be fertilized. Foliage plants only need fertilizing once a month or every six weeks during their growing season (usually October through March). Flowering plants should be fed just as they begin to bloom and approximately every two weeks thereafter.

(list continued on next page)

CARING FOR HOUSEPLANTS

Re-potting

A plant needs to be transferred to a new pot if it has outgrown its present pot to the point where the roots can no longer expand. Two common indications that it's time to re-pot a plant are 1) when roots start growing through the hole in the bottom of the pot, and 2) when the soil of a healthy plant does not seem to retain water when you water the plant.

Plants should be re-potted into a pot that is one size larger than the old pot. To re-pot a plant, first put one hand over the top of the old pot, with the main stem of the plant between your middle and index fingers. Turn the pot upside down and knock it sharply against the edge of a table. This will loosen the pot from the soil, enabling you to pull it off. Remove as much dirt as you can from between the roots and cut back any roots that appear to be broken, discolored, or rotted. After placing a piece of broken pot over the drainage hole in the new pot to keep the soil from rushing out, pour enough sterilized potting soil into the pot so that the root ball perched on it lightly will be at least ¾" from the bottom of the pot. Pour more fresh soil around the roots. Give the pot a couple of sharp raps to help settle the soil—soil should be firmly packed. Then plunge the new planting into a bucket of lukewarm water for five minutes. Your plant is now re-potted and shouldn't need to be re-potted again for about two years.

If you want to cut down on the expense of purchasing new plants, you might try swapping cuttings with friends or neighbors or attempt *garbage gardening.*

Garbage gardening involves growing plants from seeds. Use the pit from a ripe avocado, seeds from citrus foods and grapes, or sprouts on sweet potatoes. Here are some easy instructions for garbage gardening.

INSTRUCTIONS FOR GARBAGE GARDENING

Planting Avocado Pits

To plant an avocado pit, first peel away the parchment-like covering. Next, cut a tiny slice from both ends. Prop the pit, pointed end up, halfway into a glass of water, using toothpicks stuck into the pit. Three should do it. When a healthy root system has developed and a 6" sprout has emerged from the top, plant it in a pot 10" in diameter with half of the pit exposed. Then, cut the sprout back by half its length. This won't hurt your fledgling plant; in fact, you'll have a healthier, bushier plant in the long run. During its first months of growth, it's a good idea to pinch away the new leaves of every other new growth to encourage bushiness. Otherwise, you'll have a straight stalk with leaves waving from the top. It is possible to grow an avocado tree using this method.

Citrus Plants

Plant citrus seeds in a 6" pot filled with soil to an inch below the top. Soak the soil, then push about eight seeds into the soil to about ¼" deep. Keep the pot in a sunny spot and keep the soil evenly moist. When the plants begin to crowd each other, transplant them to individual pots. Citrus plants can grow to tree-size proportions and their blossoms have a light, enjoyable fragrance.

Sweet Potatoes

For a bushy sweet potato vine, choose a sweet potato with a live sprout. Suspend the potato, large end up, in a container and cover the bottom half with water. Keep it well-watered and it will rapidly grow thick with vines.

For real green thumbs, a complete book on indoor gardening and house plants is a must. They're widely available today, thanks to the popularity of house plants and indoor gardening.

BUYING A CAR

Buying and maintaining a car is a huge expense. You must carefully assess your needs to determine if there is an alternate way for you to get around. Consider mass transit or renting a car for the occasions when you really must have one.

If you live in an area where a car is a must or you're really set on having one for personal reasons, consider the following expenses of car ownership.

EXPENSES INVOLVED IN OWNING A CAR

- **Initial purchase price.** Be sure to calculate the net price of the car, dealer preparation fees, taxes, and the cost of the license and registration.
- **Financing costs.** These are computed by subtracting the down-payment (and trade-in allowance, if any) from the total purchase price and adding on the interest charges. Even if you don't borrow money for a car, the interest you lose by not having your money in a savings account is a cost of financing your purchase.
- **Depreciation.** The day you drive your new car home, it is worth less than you paid for it. Depreciation is the difference between the purchase price of the car and the value of the car if it is sold after you have used it.
- **Insurance.** Auto insurance is increasingly expensive. It can cost several hundred or several thousand dollars each year. It's especially high for city dwellers and young males.
- **Garage and Parking Lots.** In high-density areas, these may be hard to find and expensive to obtain.
- **Maintenance and Repair.** In addition to routine maintenance, you have to put money aside for those emergencies that frequently arise. Tires, batteries, shock absorbers, mufflers, and other parts will need replacing sooner or later, oil, oil filters, spark plugs, and coils need replacing regularly.
- **Gasoline.** The price of gas is skyrocketing. Calculate about how many miles you will need to drive each week and the average number of miles per gallon your car gets. This will give you a rough estimate of your basic fuel cost.
- **Miscellaneous costs.** There are little expenses such as tolls, and washing and waxing your car, which don't seem like much until you add them up on a yearly basis.

Before buying a car you should ask yourself a few basic questions:

1. *What is the maximum amount of money I am willing to spend?* Establish this figure based on (a) how much money you can afford to put down and (b) your monthly income less all other financial responsibilities. Don't exceed this figure unless you're assured of an increase in income at some definite point in the future.
2. *What car size is best for me?* Estimate the average passenger and baggage load that your car should accommodate. Too much car is unnecessary, costly, and unecological.
3. *What model interests me the most?* Check *Consumer Reports* to find how well that model performs.
4. *What features and options do I require?* Remember that every extra takes energy, and that decreases the number of miles per gallon your car can deliver.
5. *What is the delivery time? Can I wait that long?*

TYPES OF NEW CARS

Subcompact: Very small. Usually costs less to run. Convenient for short trips and around town. Not good for long trips. Front seat accommodates two adults comfortably. Rear seat is fine for children, cramped for adults. Ride is noisy, often rough. Baggage space is small. Fuel economy is excellent.

Compact: Can accommodate four adults comfortably. You can squeeze in a fifth if necessary. Generally, shorter and narrower than an intermediate. Ride is not as smooth as that of an intermediate.

Intermediate: Slightly shorter than a full-size car. A good choice is a 6-cylinder model—it only gives up 2 miles per gallon to the compacts but offers a better ride. Four-door models can realistically accommodate six passengers. Trunk room is ample.

Full-size: Six passenger car, very good for long trips. Good trunk space. Uses a lot of fuel and gets relatively few miles to the gallon. In congested areas parking is more difficult. Maneuverability is considerably less than with smaller cars.

If a new car is beyond your reach and you're considering the purchase of a used car, make sure you shop carefully before buying. Check dealer ads regularly. This will give you a good idea of current market values. Advertisements placed by private owners are not an accurate barometer.

Take into consideration a car's advantages (low mileage, useful options such as a radio, good condition). Subtract from its apparent value any needed repairs. Check for wear on tires, unrepaired or poorly repaired body damages, ease in starting, signs of body rust, and general handling. If the interior of the car is in good condition, it may mean the entire car was treated with care.

If you have a choice between buying your used car from a new or a used car company, preference should be given to the new car dealer. He maintains a service shop and has a larger investment in his business. Keep in mind that a used car dealer gets many cars from new car dealers, and often the new car dealer is letting them go because they are not completely desirable.

Whether you purchase a new or a used car, you will be required to purchase insurance. There are different types of coverage. See table on page 209.

Automobile Clubs

These clubs are useful if you own a car. For an annual fee, they supply services such as emergency towing, lists of reputable repair services, and discounts at certain motels and other facilities, as well as up-to-date information on travel conditions and preferred routes for any trip you may be planning.

Renting A Car

If you're planning to rent a car when you need it rather than purchasing one, there are a few things you should know.

INSURING YOUR CAR

Type of Coverage	Description
No-fault	Covers personal injury only, regardless of who caused the accident; covers only persons who are covered by a no-fault policy. No-fault is required in some states but not in others. Your insurance agent can tell you what is required in your state.
Family Policy	Protects you against negligence claims whether you are driving your own car or someone else's. Protection covers members of your household when they drive your car, or someone else who is driving it with your permission.
Liability Coverage	Liability coverage is quoted as a series of three numbers; e.g. 10/20/5. Add three zeros to each number. The first ($10,000) refers to the maximum payment for an injury to one person. The second number ($20,000) refers to the maximum payment for all injuries incurred in one accident. The third number ($5,000) refers to maximum payment on the property damage. Recommended minimum by Consumer Union: 25/50/10.
Medical	Pays for the medical, hospital and/or funeral expenses of accident victims. Some policies in certain states may also have wage loss benefits.
Uninsured Motorist Coverage	Protects you and your passengers in the case of an accident caused by the negligence driving of an uninsured party or a hit-and-run driver.
Collision	Insurance company will pay for damages caused by an accident. Many policies have a deductible clause. Let's assume your policy is a $100 deductible. That means you pay for the first $100 in repairs. Beyond this, your insurance company pays up to the maximum of your policy.
Comprehensive	Pays you if your car is stolen, damaged by fire, vandalism, hurricane, most noncollison causes.

In order to rent a car from most agencies, you will need a valid driver's license, one or two other proofs of your identity, at least one year in your present job, and a deposit that can range from $50 to $200. (If you're paying for the car by credit card, the deposit is usually waived.) Some agencies also have a minimum age requirement of 25 years.

In order to ensure that a car of the size you want will be available on the day you need it, make sure to call for a reservation well in advance. During peak periods, such as holidays and vacation months, rental cars can be scarce.

ONE FINAL THOUGHT

The information in this guide is meant to help you assume responsibility for your independence and avoid unnecessary and costly mistakes in coping with everyday life.

Accept the challenge of independence and enjoy the privileges of independent living. It really can be wonderful!

INDEX

A

Adult classes, 165
Annuities, 134-135
Antique shops, buying furniture in, 26
Apartments, 16-19
    building maintenance, 19
    extra services, 19
    fixtures, 18
    leases, 19-20
    light and location, 17
    room size, 17
    ventilation, 18
    See also Housing needs.
Aquarium, 201
Auction, buying furniture at, 25
Automobiles, 206-210
    buying, 206-208
    clubs, 208
    expenses in owning, 206
    insurance, 209
    questions to ask before buying, 207
    renting, 208, 210
    types of, 207-208
Avocado pits, planting, 205

B

Banking, 118-121
Bedroom furniture, 24
Beef roasting chart, 80
Biotin, 40
Birds, as pets, 200
Blindstitch, 109
Bonds, 137-138
Brunch, 158-159
Budget
    for furniture buying, 24-27
    setting up, 4-5
Buffet, 158
Building attendants, 16
Building extras, 19
Building maintenance, 19
Bulletin boards, 16
Burglary, 32-33
    tips to prevent, 33
Buttons, sewing on, 106-107

C

Calcium, 40
Calorie counter, 184-192
Carbohydrates, 36
Cars. *See* Automobiles.
Catchstitch, 108
Cats, as pets, 199-200
Charitable organizations, meeting people in, 164
Checking accounts, 119-120
Cheese, buying, 58
Cheese chart, 59-63
Cholesterol, 37
Choline, 40
Citrus plants, planting, 205
Clothing, 90-109
    basic repairs, 106-107
    care of, 96-100
    European sizes compared with American, 177
    to fit the figure, 92
    hemming a garment, 107-109
    labels, 94-96
    laundering, 101, 102
    putting together a wardrobe, 93-94

shopping for, 91-96
special care items, 101, 103
stains, removing, 103-105
for travel, 173, 177
Cocktail parties, 159
Common stock, 137
Community complexes, 10-11
Comparison shopping, 25
Condominiums, 12
Cooking, 69-85
foreign terms, 77-79
ingredients commonly used, 75-77
methods of, 79-85
terms and abbreviations, 70-74
Cooperatives, 12
Credit
types of, 122-123
standing (how to check), 128-132
worthiness, 124-125
Credit cards
cost of, 125-126
do's and don't's of, 127-128
how to get, 125
liability in case of loss, 126
types of, 123-124
Customs information, 176-178
Cyanocobalamine (B-12), 40

D

Decor (apartment), 23-24
Dental care, 194
Diets, reducing, 183
Dining area furniture, 25
Dishes, washing, 160
Doctors, 193
Documents and papers, keeping, 147, 148
Dogs, as pets, 198-199
Doors, securing, 31

E

Emergency telephone numbers, 34
Endowment policies, 133

Entertaining at home, 151-160
and cleaning up, 160
key to success, 151-153
See also Parties.
Exercise, 180, 181

F

Fair Credit Reporting Act, 128, 129, 130
Fiber care chart, 97-100
Fire precautions, 33-34
Fish
buying, 57
as pets, 200-201
Flea market, buying furniture in, 26
Folacin, 39-40
Food, 35-89
calorie counter, 184-192
cooking, 69-85
five basic groups, 41
kitchen safety, 87-89
menu planning, 41
nutrition, 36-40
recommended daily amounts, 44
serving, 86-87
shopping for, 41-69
Food safety, 89
Food shopping, 41-69
cheese, 58-63
do's and don't's of, 45-46
herbs and spices, 64-67
meat, poultry, and fish, 47-57
rules for, 41-45
selecting quality items, 46
unpacking purchases, 69
vegetables and fruit, 57
Fruit, buying, 57
Furniture, buying, 24-27
on a budget, 25-27

G

Garage sale, buying furniture at, 26
Garbage gardening, 205
Garden apartments, 10

Goodwill Industry, 26-27
Gourmet cooking, foreign terms used, 77-79

H

Ham baking chart, 83
Health, 179-194
    calorie counter, 184-192
    dental care, 194
    desirable weights, 182
    exercise, 180, 181
    finding a doctor, 193
    getting in shape, 180-183
    insurance, 135-136
    precautions when traveling, 172
    professionals, 194-196
Hemming a garment, 107-109
Herb and spice chart, 65-67
Herbs and spices, 64
High-rise buildings, 10
Housekeeping, 27-30
    basic supplies, 28
    cleaning guide, 29
    outside help, 29-30
House plants, 202-205
    caring for, 203-204
    garbage gardening, 205
    light required for, 203
Housewares, buying, 27
Housing needs, 8-34
    buying a home, 11-12
    emergency telephone numbers, 34
    finding a place to live, 9-13
    fire precautions, 33-34
    furnishings, 24-27
    "good" apartment (what to look for), 16-19
    housekeeping, 27-30
    leases, 19-20
    moving in, 20-22
    planning the decor, 23-24
    renting, 10-11
    resources, 15-16
    roommates, 14-15
    security precautions, 30-33

I

Independent living, 2-7
    costs of, 3
    decision for, 2-3
    lifestyle checklist, 3
    monthly expenses, 6-7
    place to live, 8-34
    setting up a budget, 4-5
Insurance, 132-136
    annuities, 134-135
    automobile, 209
    health, 135-136
    life, 132-134
Investments, 136-140
    bonds, 137-138
    securities, 136
    stocks, 137, 138-139
Iron, 40

J

Jobs, 111-114
    application and interview, 114
    how to find, 111-113
    résumé, 113

K

Kitchen abbreviations (in cooking), 70
Kitchen safety, 87-89

L

Labels, clothing, 94-96
Lamb, buying, 56
Lamb broiling chart, 82
Lamb roasting chart, 82
Laundry, 101, 102
Lawyer, 144-145
Leases, 19-20
    questions to ask before signing, 20
Legal Aid Society, 146

INDEX   **213**

Legalities, 144-149
    finding a good lawyer, 144-145
    keeping documents and papers, 147, 148
    power of attorney, 146
    suing in Small Claims Court, 145-146
    wills, 147-149
Leisure time, 150-178
    at-home entertaining, 151-160
    meeting people, 162-166
    travel, 166-178
Life insurance, 132-134
Lifestyle, checklist for, 3
Limited payment life policy, 133
Living room furniture, 24
Loans, bank, 121
Locks, 31-32

M

Meat
    buying, 47
    carving, 86
    grades of, 47
Menu
    dinner party, 154
    planning, 41
Metric system, 176
Minerals, 40, 43
Mobile homes, 12
Money management, 110-149
    banking basics, 118-121
    career choice and, 111-114
    computing monthly expenses, 6-7
    credit and credit cards, 122-132
    insurance, 132-136
    investments, 136-140
    legal matters, 144-149
    stretching the dollar, 115-118
    taxes, 140-144
    when traveling, 171
Moving, 20-22
    checklist for, 21-22
Mutton, buying, 56

N

Neighbors, meeting, 165
Newspaper advertisements, for finding an apartment, 15
Niacin (B-3), 39
Nutrients, 36-40

O

Oven safety, 88
Oven temperatures, 71
Over-the-counter stocks, 139-140

P

Pantothenic acid, 39
Parties, 153-160
    "Bring Your Own," 160
    brunch, 158-159
    buffet, 158
    cocktail party, 159
    dinner party, 153-157
    theme party, 159
Passport, how to obtain, 171-172
People, meeting, 162-166
    adult classes, 165
    friends of friends, 162
    neighbors, 165
    in politics, 164
    religious and charitable organizations, 164
    singles' bars, 165-166
    singles' clubs, 164
    sports participation, 165
    when traveling, 163-164
    at work, 163
Pets, owning, 198-202
    aquarium, 200-201
    birds, 200
    cats, 199-200
    dogs, 198-199
    responsibility for, 198
    wildlife or unusual pets, 201-202
Place to live
    how to choose, 9

needs and, 13
types of rentals available, 10-12
See also Housing needs.
Politics, meeting people in, 164
Pork, buying, 56
Pork roasting chart, 80
Poultry
    buying, 47
    carving, 86-87
    cooking, 84
Power of attorney, 146
Preferred stock, 137
Protein, 36
Pyridoxine (B-6), 39

R

Real estate agents, 16
Recommended Dietary Allowances (RDA's), 36, 40, 41, 42, 43
Red meat, cooking, 80-83
Reinforced buttons, 107
Religious organizations, meeting people in, 164
Résumé (job), 113
Retail Merchants Association, 25
Retirement income policy, 134
Riboflavin (B-2), 39
Rider (lease), 19
Roommates, 14-15
Room rentals, 11
Rummage sales, buying furniture at, 26

S

Salvation Army, 26-27
Savings accounts, 121
Seafood, cooking methods for, 85
Seafood chart (seasonal), 57
Securities, types of, 136
Securities and Exchange Commission (SEC), 139
Security precautions, 30-33
    doors, 31
    safety rules, 30
    windows, 32

Self-evaluation, 2
Serving food, 86-87
Sew-through buttons, 106
Shank buttons, 107
Shopping
    for clothes, 91-96
    for food, 41-69
    traditional sale periods, 116
Single-family homes, 11
Singles' bars, 165-166
Singles' clubs, 164
Small Claims Court, 144-145
Snaps and hooks and eyes, 106, 107
Sodium, 37
Soundproofing an apartment, 18
Sports participation (and meeting people), 165
Stains, removing from clothing, 103-105
Staples, food, 68
Stocks
    commission on transactions, 138
    common and preferred, 137
    dealing with a broker, 139
    listed and over-the-counter, 139-140
    trading of, 138
Straight life policy, 133
Studio apartments (efficiencies), 17
Sweet potatoes, planting, 205

T

Taxes, 140-144
    commonly asked questions, 141-143
    filing, 141
    forms, 140
    preparing, 140
    shelter annuities, 134
    tips on, 144
Term insurance policies, 133
Thiamin (B-1), 39
Tipping, 117-118

Tourist offices (foreign government), 169-170
Townhouse apartments, 10
Travel, 166-178
    alone or with a friend, 167
    arranging the trip, 168
    clothing for, 173, 177
    customs information, 176-178
    deciding where to go, 168
    health precautions, 172
    luggage, 173-174
    and meeting people, 163-164
    metric equivalents, 176
    money management, 171
    obtaining a passport, 171-172
    preparing to leave, 172-173
    tips on, 175
    useful abbreviations, 174
Two family homes, 11

U

Underwriter's Laboratory (UL), 33
Used-furniture stores, 26-27

V

Variable annuity, 134
Veal, buying, 56
Veal roasting chart, 80
Vegetables, buying, 57
Ventilation, apartment, 18
Vitamins, 37-40, 42
    A (retinol), 38
    B vitamins, 39-40
    C (ascorbic acid), 38
    D, 38
    E, 38-39

W

Weekend brunches, 158-159
Weights, desirable, 182
Weights and measures, table of, 70
Wildlife pets, 201-202
Wills, 147-149
Windows, securing, 32
Wine, 155-157
    glossary, 157
    selecting, 156
    serving, 155